ON-LEASH AGGRESSION

TRIGGERS AND REACTIONS: A GUIDE TO FIXING DOG BEHAVIOR PROBLEMS

VOLUME 1
ON-LEASH AGGRESSION

JEFF MILLMAN, CTC

TRIGGERS AND REACTIONS: A GUIDE TO FIXING DOG BEHAVIOR PROBLEMS, VOLUME 1: ON-LEASH AGGRESSION

Copyright 2024 © Jeff Millman Dog training, LLC

ISBN 979-8-9895814-0-5

JEFF MILLMAN DOG TRAINING, LLC
CARY, NC
UNITED STATES
WWW.JEFFMILLMAN.COM

Author: Jeff Millman
Art Direction: Jeff Millman
Graphic Design: Jeff Millman
Layout: Jeff Millman
Cover Design: Jeff Millman with Midjourney
Illustrations: Jeff Millman with Midjourney
Editing: Jeff Millman with many wonderful friends and family

TABLE OF CONTENTS

DEDICATION

To all the dogs out there that are just trying to be the best versions of themselves. They need our help to provide love, guidance, compassion, exercise and patience.

It is not a dog's responsibility to be human. It is our responsibility to understand that dogs are complex, wonderful animals and we are lucky to have them in our lives. It is a privilege, not a right to have a dog.

FROM JEAN DONALDSON

"Jeff has packed this book with practical advice and education for guardians of reactive dogs. He has compassion not just for dogs but for his human clients and it shines through on every page. Concerned always with the underlying emotions and motivations, the solutions go much deeper than improving manners."

Jean Donaldson is the Founder, Principal Instructor, Coach and Mentor of The Academy for Dog Trainers.

Author of *The Culture Clash, Mine! A Guide to Resource Guarding in Dogs, Fight! A Guide to Dog-Dog Aggression, Dogs Are From Neptune,* and *Oh Behave! Dogs From Pavlov to Premack to Pinker* and *Train Like a Pro* and *Dog Training 101* for The Great Courses.

ACKNOWLEDGEMENTS

I have a ton of thanks to give. Writing this book took a lot of time and energy, and I could not have done it without the support of family and friends.

Cassy, my amazing wife, along with my two wonderful kids, showed incredible patience and support while I spent endless hours writing and editing.

I also want to thank many friends and family that helped by reading my book, giving encouragement and help with editing.

Kalli Connor, Marisa Evans, Helen Herber, Joel Koplos, Don Millman, Nona Millman, Christina Taylor, Meaghan Tower and Josh Waller

I want to give special thanks to Jean Donaldson for her amazing dog training school, The Academy for Dog Trainers, that I attended in 2002, and her continued help and encouragement since then.

INTRODUCTION

Leash aggression is the primary focus of this book. The term "aggression" represents not only barking, growling and biting, but any undesired reactivity. As you read through the pages of this book, you could replace "aggression" with "reactivity" and everything would still make sense.

Your dog might not be dangerous, but he or she may exhibit other undesired leash reactions such as whining or pulling towards other dogs. I will teach you how to fix your dog's undesired leash reactions. This book can help if you are afraid to take your dog for a walk because they might bite a dog or a person, or embarrassed because your barking, whining, friendly dog is socially awkward and does not know how to greet other dogs politely.

This book synthesizes over twenty-one years of knowledge from working closely with thousands of dogs of all ages, breeds, temperaments, and learning styles. I appreciate and understand that all dogs are unique in some ways, but similar in some ways as well. Dogs don't play dead when they are under duress. They don't dig a hole and hide. All dogs possess a predetermined range of behaviors. Not every dog responds in exactly the same way, but every dog pulls from the same list of responses.

Once you understand how to read your dog's emotional state and respond in the correct way, your dog's stress levels will decrease. If their stress levels decrease, their reactivity will decrease as well.

Throughout the pages of this book, you will learn the science behind dog reactivity, how to analyze and reduce it, why desensitization is the best option, and why obedience is not. I will show you specific step-by-step strategies to lower reactivity, whether your dog is excited and wild, or fearful and aggressive. Daily, I deal with dogs that bark, snarl, lunge, and bite. Through my work with thousands of dogs, I have found the formula for success and I am thrilled to share it with you.

You can grab a coffee and read the entire book, or you can read a bit, practice the exercises and come back for more strategies and tips.

Caution is always the most important focus when dealing with reactivity. You should be careful that you are keeping your dog and everyone else safe and comfortable. Keep in mind you will have a much smoother experience if the exercises seem boring and uneventful.

I am glad you are here.

Sincerely,
Jeff Millman, CTC

Chapter 1
LEASH AGGRESSION

🐾

To help your dog be less reactive, your primary goal should be to lower your dog's stress near triggers. A trigger is something in the environment that your dog notices. The stress caused by a trigger can lead to an undesired behavior change.

No one ever hires me if their dog simply *looks* at a trigger. I get hired to change a dog's undesired reaction to triggers such as barking, jumping, lunging, growling, or biting. The key is to lower the intensity of your dog's response to triggers so your dog remains calm.

You can change your dog's behavior if you know how to *desensitize* your dog to triggers. A calm dog simply looks at something or ignores it and doesn't react in an undesired way. Keep your dog calm and the undesired behaviors go away. To *desensitize* a dog to something is to make him non-reactive. A *sensitized* dog is extra sensitive or reactive.

When my family and I lived in Chicago, we lived in a townhome on a very busy street. We had a small fenced-in yard and three dogs; two Collies and a Sheltie. If you know herding dogs, you know they react to movement. I worked diligently to desensitize our dogs to people and dogs walking by our home. From our dining room overlooking the yard, we found it quite humorous watching pedestrians walk by, stop, and look in our yard.

They would look at our dogs with confused looks on their faces as my dogs calmly looked back at them. Most dogs in the neighborhood would charge their fence or bark at people going by. Our dogs were quiet and did not react. I desensitized them to movement, people and dogs. Desensitization can work if you are diligent and understand the cause and effect of triggers.

BUILDUP OF STRESS CAUSES FRUSTRATION

Stress is a physiological response to a trigger. Repeated stress causes more sensitivity to triggers and more reactivity. If stress continues to build, a dog will also get frustrated and react more strongly towards the trigger and his behaviors will be more extreme. If a dog barks out of the window at each passing dog, by the end of the day, his frustration will increase, and he will intensify his barking since it is not achieving his desired outcome. The escalation of behaviors will occur whether a dog wants to play with or attack each passing dog.

PHYSICAL AND MENTAL STIMULATION ARE IMPORTANT

Every dog needs a certain amount of physical exercise each day to be relaxed and cheerful. They also need some type of mental exercise using food puzzles or training sessions, as well. Most people default to providing their dog physical exercise if they think their dog is bored. That is important, but dogs that receive proper physical exercise and are not mentally challenged can have behavior problems.

3-HOUR VISLA

In Chicago, I received a desperate call from a prospective client named Steve. He had a two-year-old Visla that was stressing him out. Steve was very active, was a marathon runner, and had many dogs in the past. He told me that even though he exercised his dog for three hours each day, his dog was ripping up furniture and seemed anxious and would not calm down at home. I asked Steve how much training he gives his dog each day. He informed me he practiced training with his dog when he was a puppy, but doesn't do much training now.

I recommended he cut back on his dog's physical exercise by sixty minutes daily, and allocate thirty minutes for training. I told him to reach out again in two weeks and report if there was any change in his dog's behavior. It surprised him I was suggesting *less* time each day overall, but I told him I think it will solve his problem. He contacted me after two weeks and was thrilled with the outcome. He told me his dog sleeps during the day, is much calmer and hasn't destroyed anything in over a week. As I suspected, his dog was physically tired and mentally bored. Once Steve found the correct balance of physical and mental exercise, his dog was happy and tired.

Dogs typically need a minimum of sixty minutes of physical exercise and fifteen minutes of training, or mental exercise every day. Some dogs need a lot more than this. If you have a Visla, German Shepherd, any herding dog or working breed, your dog might need a lot more than those recommendations. Dogs usually calm down a bit by two years of age, but some dogs are incredibly high energy until they are much older.

TIRED DOGS ARE LESS AGGRESSIVE

Getting outside help, such as hiring dog walkers or enrolling your dog in training classes or activities, can help keep your dog relaxed. In addition, necessary stimulation can be achieved through added time with food puzzles, safe chew options, and snuffle mats. Any treatment for aggression will be easier if your dog is receiving their daily dose of activity.

Using this book's desensitization techniques will mentally stimulate, and tire your dog, benefiting them while treating aggression. Just keeping dogs under threshold and calm will make them more tired and relaxed.

As you work through the strategies of this book, notice that your dog is more relaxed, happier, and tired. Everything becomes easier once you figure out what your dog needs and how to provide it to her. Try to avoid fighting your dog's needs. It will get easier.

Chapter 2
PREVENT NEGATIVE GENERALIZATION

🐾

Prospective clients often contact me when their dog's behavior worsens. They will explain that their dog used to go nose-to-nose and sniff dogs without incident, or used to love getting petted by the neighbor. Now their dog barks across the street at other dogs or growls at the neighbor. Their dog is more stressed, the reactivity is more extreme and appearing at a farther distance. What happened?

Stress is the body's natural response to challenging situations or changes in the environment. Anxiety is the fear or apprehension of perceived threats. If a dog is attacked at a dog park, they might become *anxious* when they are near the park or even just hear dogs barking.

When dogs get more reactive, the most likely explanation is that the dog generalized their anxiety to more triggers. I refer to it as "anxious about getting anxious." Previously, the dog was calm when she was five feet, three feet, two feet, etc. away from another dog, but sometimes it ended badly for her and she got stressed. Now, she sees another dog at twenty feet away and she anticipates what can happen as she gets closer and she becomes nervous sooner. Instead of being anxious solely about touching noses with another dog, she is anxious about dogs *in general*. This causes stress to increase sooner and results in more extreme reactions to triggers. Increased tension results in rapid responses.

If you've noticed your dog's stress escalating and a situation worsening, the solution lies in gradually exposing your dog to triggers at manageable distances and intensity levels. By accumulating positive experiences, you can reverse the anxiety and eventually increase the intensity of the trigger while keeping her calm. Don't rush the process, or it could cause emotional setbacks and undo progress.

THIS IS NOT OBEDIENCE

Wherever your dog's stress level currently registers, I want to show you how to lower it using simple, humane strategies. Keep in mind that reducing your dog's stress levels is **not obedience**. You can't tell your dog to "be calm" around something that she intensely reacts to. It doesn't work. It is a waste of time. You also should not ask your dog to "Sit," "Watch Me," "Quiet," "Lie Down," or another request.

Consider this: your dog barks at a passing dog. You ask her to "Sit," block her view, or ask her to face you, all at the same distance from the other dog where she first barked to show discomfort and ask it to go away. You asked her to put herself in a more vulnerable position at the same distance that she showed discomfort. This can spike her stress levels. Often dogs under duress won't sit, won't take treats, and have no other option but to be more obvious in their signals by growling, barking or biting.

"You want me to sit and
ignore that scary dog?"

This amount of stress can lead dogs to become overwhelmed by intense fear **(*flooding*),** or if they frequently face stress and bad situations, they might feel powerless over their surroundings and stop trying (*learned helplessness*). In both cases, you can misinterpret their behavior as "being good" when they are simply too afraid to tell anyone that something is causing them stress. You can also misinterpret their behavior as "being bad" if they bark when, in fact, they are simply acting defensively.

In those situations, your dog is too nervous or frustrated to calm down and perform a behavior on cue. The only way to calm your dog down is to remove your dog or remove the trigger. If you don't move your dog away, she is forced to communicate her escalating discomfort by being more obvious and possibly growling, barking or biting.

Rather than expecting your dog to obey a command, remove her from that situation and desensitize her to triggers that cause stress, like seeing or hearing other dogs. Understanding triggers and how to address them is critical to your success.

USE OBEDIENCE TO EVALUATE STRESS, NOT FIX IT

It is best to desensitize your dog to other dogs before asking her to perform a specific behavior in a highly charged situation. Then, once your dog seems more calm, use obedience to evaluate whether your dog is actually calm. If you think she is calm, ask her to "sit" or perform another behavior. If she performs that behavior without hesitation, it's a sign that the surrounding activity, like dogs, people, and skateboards, isn't causing her stress.

But, as the environment changes, it is important to check in with her and see if she is still calm. If she is calm with another dog twenty feet away, what happens if that dog barks? What happens if he comes one foot closer? It is important to understand that subtle changes in the environment can trigger a dog to react. Stay vigilant and frequently reevaluate your dog's comfort level.

DO NOT PUNISH REACTIONS

Sadly, some trainers may suggest choking, shocking or "correcting" a reactive dog who barks or growls to quiet them. Fortunately, more people recognize the harm of these strategies and are seeking kinder alternatives.

I am grateful when a dog displays his discomfort with me by growling instead of looking calm and immediately biting me. "Thanks for telling me you are not comfortable. No problem, I will move away and we can work at a farther distance!"

If you punish growling, barking or snarling, then your dog will still feel stressed, but might be afraid to tell anyone. Then, you have a scared dog that might skip warning signals and immediately resort to biting. Sometimes, dogs that bite without warning cannot be rehabilitated because there are limited ways to track their progress during treatment.

Respect your dog's subtle signals by moving your dog away from the stress-inducing trigger. You will have much more success this way. You don't want to ignore his signals, so he has to bark, growl, show teeth, or bite before someone gives him space.

EVALUATE AND ADJUST TO YOUR DOG'S STRESS

You should focus on lowering your dog's stress so he is calm or happy around the trigger. Not because you *told him* to, but because he doesn't *feel* stressed. Even the most reactive dog can be calm at a certain distance from another dog, person or noise and not react. At this distance, the trigger does not cause stress. It does not cause a fight-or-flight response.

During my time in Chicago, I worked with a 90-pound German Shepherd who was extremely reactive in the presence of other dogs. He was so frustrated that he could not be closer to the other dog that he would attack whoever held the leash. He had to bite *something*. That type of reactivity is called *redirected aggression* and shows a high level of frustration and agitation. While most dogs may not experience such high levels of stress, your task is to identify your dog's comfort level and work at the correct distance.

SUMMARY

- Stress and anxiety are common factors contributing to a dog's reactivity. Stress is the body's reaction to triggers, while anxiety is worrying about dangers.
- Both fear or frustration both contribute to escalating stress levels and reactivity.
- Dogs can become more reactive over time if they generalize their anxiety to more triggers. This makes them anticipate stress even from far away.
- Improve a reactive dog's behavior by gradually exposing them to triggers in a positive way, starting from a safe distance.
- Lowering high levels of stress cannot be achieved through obedience commands; instead, it involves recognizing subtle signals and moving the dog away from stress-inducing triggers and desensitizing him to those triggers.
- Obedience commands can be used to evaluate if your dog is calm, not to reduce stress in a highly agitated dog.

Chapter 3
UNDERSTANDING TRIGGERS

🐾

Dogs react to individual triggers, but it is important to understand how combining triggers can cause unexpected, extreme behavior changes.

STACKED TRIGGERS

Dogs may react to a single trigger, like seeing a dog or hearing a door knock, or multiple triggers happening together. *Stacked Triggers* are multiple triggers that happen simultaneously that cause a dog to have an extreme reaction. If there was just one trigger at a time, the reaction would be less severe.

For instance, let's say a dog guards his dog bed, guards his bone, is not comfortable with toddlers and doesn't enjoy being petted on his head. If a toddler pets a dog while he's chewing on a bone and lying on his bed, it might cause an instant severe reaction, and even a bite. One trigger may have caused the dog to stiffen, growl or bark, but the combination of triggers can cause an intense, immediate response.

COMPOUND TRIGGERS

If dogs are exposed to many stressors without enough time to recover, their reactions can seem inconsistent and extreme.

Let's say a dog chases cats, is afraid of firetrucks, and is nervous around male joggers when they are too close.

Over the course of a fifteen-minute walk that dog hears a fire truck rumble by, sees a cat shortly after that and that resulting stress causes the dog to nip the leg of a jogger running by. Triggers were not stacked since they did not happen simultaneously, but the dog's stress ramped up because of multiple triggers in a short period without enough recovery time.

Would your dog bark at this?

This resulted in the buildup of stress and caused a more extreme reaction. It is important to work on each trigger that causes reactivity, so your dog's stress does not go unchecked and build to a bite.

CORTISOL AND REACTIVITY

Cortisol, commonly known as the "stress hormone," affects a dog's reactivity. When dogs encounter triggers, their bodies release cortisol as part of the stress response. The presence of cortisol in the bloodstream prepares the dog for a "fight or flight" response, which can lead to increased reactivity.

Cortisol levels can increase rapidly and stay at an increased level for a long time after a stressful event, making treatment more difficult. It makes sense if you think about it: A dog perceives a dog in view as a serious threat. His cortisol levels rise since now he is in fight-or-flight mode. Even when the other dog is out of sight, the nervous dog is still on high alert, worried the other dog might return. He needs to stay vigilant and be on guard. If another trigger appears during this time, his cortisol levels will rise again.

This pattern leads to a less tolerant, more reactive dog and causes a lot of strain on all parts of the body, which is not healthy. If your dog's reactivity escalates and he becomes more easily triggered, it may be best to take him home. Learn from that situation and try to avoid putting him over his threshold in the future.

MEDICATION OPTIONS TO REDUCE STRESS

Giving dogs over-the-counter options like Solliquin, or prescription medication options like Prozac, can help lower anxiety and reactivity, making desensitization more effective. This topic is not a new, unproven science or something that

15

should cause you undue worry. I suggest you discuss these options with your veterinarian or Veterinary Behaviorist. While not a quick fix, the correct medication can make treatment easier.

I urge you to consider medication for your dog if you are having difficulty using desensitization alone to lower stress. Desensitization is the best option to treat anxiety and aggression. But, if dogs get extremely agitated every walk and they also do not calm down quickly, treatment can be difficult, if not impossible.

SUMMARY

- Stacked Triggers: Multiple triggers occurring simultaneously can lead to severe reactions in dogs.
- Compound Triggers: Accumulated stress from multiple triggers over time can cause inconsistent and extreme reactions.
- By addressing triggers individually and using effective management techniques, we can prevent stress and extreme reactions in dogs.
- Cortisol and Reactivity: Cortisol, the stress hormone, affects dog reactivity and can lead to prolonged stress.
- Veterinarians should be consulted to discuss medication options, as medication like Prozac can be beneficial in reducing reactivity in some dogs.

Chapter 4
JUST USE A CLICKER

🐾

Some training books have *Clicker* in the title. This helps distinguish them from other training books that don't reference a clicker. I left it out of the title because it's just a tool to improve your training, not a radically new strategy. I am confident once you use one, you will understand the benefits and see the results.

I assume you did not wake up this morning and say for the first time, "You know, my dog is a bit leash reactive, let me see what I can do about it." It's likely that you sought information from various sources, such as other books, trainers, friends, and online research. After all that, your dog is still reactive and here you are looking for help. That tells me that your problem is still present, and the other strategies did not work.

You need my help, so let me help you. I will not recommend you yell at your dog, hurt, pinch, choke or even talk in a loud voice to your dog. It will be humane, logical and effective. Give your dog the chance to live a less stressful life by following the strategies in this book --- and use a clicker!

I will not spend more time trying to eliminate any hesitation that might be present, but just to urge you to purchase one and start using it following my direction. Used correctly, the clicker works better than not using it. ESPECIALLY for aggression.

'CLICK' TO EVALUATE STRESS LEVELS

You can use the clicker to evaluate your dog's stress levels and comfort. Since the clicker ALWAYS means there is a treat present, you can use it to determine what captures your dog's attention. If he ignores the 'click' and continues looking at another dog, it means he is more concerned with the other dog and he then might whine, bark, or lunge. It helps you determine if your dog is calm or not. If he doesn't *care* about the other dog, he won't react. This is key when the goal is to desensitize your dog to triggers.

So, if you don't have a clicker, get a clicker. You can find them at most large pet food stores, or online. Here is an example of a box clicker.

I recommend box clickers since they are louder. If your dog is especially sound sensitive, there are versions that have a protruding "button" that are quieter. Let's do a quick exercise using the clicker to introduce this amazing tool.

EXERCISE
CHARGE THE CLICKER
Things you need:
- Your dog
- Amazing treats that your dog LOVES
- A clicker

GOAL
YOUR DOG LEARNS 'CLICK' MEANS "TREAT"
To associate the clicker with something positive, you will simply 'click' and then give your dog a treat.

THINGS TO LOOK FOR
YOUR DOG IS AFRAID OF THE CLICKER
Some dogs can be sound sensitive and can be afraid of the noise that the clicker makes. If your dog blinks each time you 'click,' backs up, tucks his tail, licks his lips or stops taking treats, these are indications he is afraid of the clicker. It's possible for dogs to develop a fear of clickers over time, so stay observant and discontinue use if your dog shows signs of fear.

If this occurs, try muffling the clicker in your pocket or under your arm. You can also stop using the clicker and just say the word "Yes!" in a clear, short tone. "Yeeeeessss," differs from "Yes!" Use the short version and be consistent.

Even if your dog is not afraid of the clicker, never 'click' too close to his ear. It is quite loud, can cause discomfort and can eventually lead to him being afraid of it.

19

If your dog is sensitive to the clicker indoors, it might be okay to use it outdoors. When indoors, the noise bounces off of the walls and ceiling and can be more intense. Try your best to get your dog used to it. Using a clicker provides a consistent evaluation strategy and can really help make training more efficient.

LET'S GET STARTED - CHARGE THE CLICKER
ONE CLICK ONE TREAT

- Watch your dog.
- 'Click' once and give your dog a treat.
- Repeat five to ten times.
- Don't worry about what your dog is doing, unless he is doing something that is not appropriate. For instance, you don't want to 'click' and treat when your dog is chewing on your rug or jumping on you.

WHEN TO STOP

When your dog consistently (and quickly) turns his head around to get the treat after the 'click,' you are done charging the clicker! It might only take three to five clicks total, or you might have to do multiple sessions.

You might do a brief session of five to ten 'clicks' a few times a day before your dog understands. You might also want to take a break if your dog simply lies down in front of you and waits for treats. It is not bad to reward a calm dog, but to really know if you have properly charged the clicker, it is helpful to see your dog quickly turn around when he hears the 'click.'

TROUBLESHOOTING TIPS

- If your dog doesn't seem interested, use better treats! I always tell my clients that they should use a treat that is so enticing that their dog doesn't leave them alone for ten minutes after they give it.
- Attempt to give a treat every time you 'click' whether your dog turns towards the clicker or not.

COMMON QUESTIONS

Do I have to use the clicker forever? No. Once your dog is consistently neutral or happy when exposed to an event, you don't have to use the clicker for that event.

Do I have to use the clicker every time, or can I say, "Yes" sometimes? You can alternate between "Yes!" and the clicker, but the clicker is more noticeable and usually works better for dogs that are not afraid of it.

Do I have to give a treat after the 'click' or "Yes"? Absolutely. Once your dog is more stable and consistent, you will 'click' and treat less frequently. However, EVERY time you 'click' or "Yes!" you will give a treat.

My dog did not turn around when I 'click,' Do I still give her a treat? Yes. Attempt to give a treat after the 'click.' It is not an obedience issue where she is being "bad" for not turning around. You can use it to evaluate where her attention lies. If she doesn't turn around immediately, it indicates that she is distracted or nervous. Use that information to decide whether you need to move her away. If she doesn't turn around, attempt to give her the treat. If she doesn't turn around *or* take the treat, move her away to a more comfortable location.

What is the clicker doing? Think of the clicker as a camera and it marks one of two things. It marks an event that you want your dog to ignore (desensitization) or a behavior that you want your dog to repeat (obedience).

Is the clicker based on science? Yes! If you are working on desensitization and marking events, you are also helping your dog enjoy the experience. This is called *Classical Conditioning*. By rewarding your dog's obedience and marking behaviors, you encourage them to repeat those behaviors. This is called *Operant Conditioning*.

How do I use the clicker for leash reactivity? You will "take a picture" of the event that your dog is experiencing. For example, 'click' as soon as your dog looks at another dog. If he is more interested in the 'click' and turns away from the dog, you are desensitizing him or teaching him not to react to that trigger. Your dog will naturally enjoy the experience more instead of being stressed or frustrated. The goal is to help your dog be calm and not react to triggers. If you are unsure of your dog's reaction to a trigger, 'click' AS SOON as your dog sees or hears the trigger. If he turns towards you without hesitation, he is not too concerned with the trigger.

Can I use the clicker for obedience? Absolutely. Think of the clicker as a camera and you are *taking a picture* of a behavior. If your dog sits and you 'click' and give a treat, you mark that behavior and reward it, increasing the chances your dog performs that behavior again. Use the clicker this way after you have determined that your dog is calm around a trigger or there are no triggers present.

Can I use the clicker to get my dog to come to me? No, it is not a remote control. You should not use it to start a behavior such as, "Come," or stop a behavior such as barking at another dog or jumping on someone.

So what do I do if my dog is barking? Great question! Move your dog away to a location where he stops barking. Wait for him to look back at the trigger and 'click.' If he turns towards the 'click' and takes the treat, it means the desensitization process has started successfully. If he ignores the 'click', doesn't turn around or doesn't take the treat, he is still anxious and you need to find another way to lower the intensity of the trigger that caused the barking. I will discuss this throughout this book. Read on!

Note: From here on out I will use 'click' and treat, but you can always use "Yes!" instead. But the clicker is louder and more consistent and simply works better! Use it when you can.

SUMMARY

- "Charging the clicker" means linking the 'click' sound to treats to create a positive association and reinforce desired behaviors or positive experiences.
- Using a clicker in dog training is a powerful and efficient tool for positive reinforcement.
- The clicker helps mark the exact moment of desired behavior, or marks the moment a dog experiences an event.
- If your dog is afraid of the 'click,' muffle the clicker or using a verbal marker -"Yes!"
- There are two ways to use the clicker: as a reward for good behavior, or to help your dog become less sensitive to triggers by clicking when they notice one.
- If your dog doesn't respond to the 'click,' first try better treats.
- Never 'click' without attempting to give a treat.

Chapter 5
EVALUATE CLICKER RESPONSE

Keep your dog calm by evaluating his stress levels and moving him to a new location if needed. Once your dog is clicker charged, he should turn around without hesitation when he hears the 'click' if he loves the treats you are using. Each time you 'click,' you can evaluate your dog's reaction to determine if he is nervous or interested.

There are two reasons a clicker-charged dog might not turn to the sound of the click:

1. He is nervous. The trigger is potentially dangerous.
2. He is more interested in the trigger. The trigger is interesting, and he wants to move closer and interact with it.

THE CLICKER PROVIDES INFORMATION

Move your dog to a new location if he is does not respond to the clicker. I will explain the step-by-step strategies later, but for now, just remember that if your dog does not respond to the clicker, you need to MOVE him to a new location.

Fearful or aggressive dogs require more caution than frustrated dogs. If your dog has shown extreme reactivity, snapped at or bitten another dog or person, you need to be extra careful around triggers.

It is important that you can evaluate how calm your dog is. Clicking and treating gives more insight into your dog's reaction than just observing your dog's body language.

The clicker is a useful tool because:

1. It helps your dog enjoy situations by pairing the situation with something wonderful.
2. It helps you to evaluate your dog's stress levels.

Use the clicker to assess the situation, make informed decisions, and be safe. ***Will you have to use the clicker forever?*** No. Until you have a deeper understanding of your dog's reactivity, the clicker and the strategies I'll provide are the best way to make well-informed safety decisions.

MISSED OPPORTUNITY

Several years ago, a client in Raleigh, North Carolina, emailed me to tell me his dog bit someone at a restaurant. I predicted what his answer was going to be, but I emailed him:

"What did your dog do when you were 'clicking' and treating as the person approached?"

As expected, he told me he did not have his clicker with him and he wasn't 'clicking' and treating. He said that his dog "seemed" fine before this incident.

Using the clicker to evaluate his dog's response could have helped him monitor his dog's stress levels and prevent the incident. Dogs rarely ramp up from a completely calm state to a bite without warning. It can happen, but is rare. If a dog bites without warning, he should not be in a restaurant setting to begin with.

When I worked with my client and his dog, I saw clear signs of stress when his dog was uncomfortable. These signs included body stiffening, delayed turning, a rough mouth when taking treats, or refusing treats. If he were monitoring his dog's reactions, he could have moved his dog away or left the restaurant all together as soon as he noticed a behavior change.

Think of the clicker as a way to ask your dog, "How distracted or nervous are you at this moment when you are looking at the person or dog in front of you?"

THE CLICKER IS NOT A REMOTE CONTROL

One important point is to understand that the clicker is not a remote control. You are not "trying" to get your dog to turn around by 'clicking,' but you are evaluating your dog's emotional response to a situation. Usually, if there's a tasty treat behind him, he *will* turn to get it after hearing the 'click.'

So, don't double click. If your dog doesn't turn around immediately after hearing the 'click,' simply move him away to a new location. When you 'click,' gather information to determine if you should keep your dog where he is, move away, or move closer to the trigger. The goal is that he can be around a trigger and be calm. Once you find the correct distance where he is comfortable, you can use that to adjust your distance the next time to avoid starting too close to a trigger.

SUMMARY
- The clicker can be used to evaluate your dog's stress levels and create positive experiences.
- If the dog turns towards you immediately after hearing the click, it indicates that he can ignore the trigger and he will not react in an undesired way.

- If your dog doesn't turn around immediately, it may suggest that the trigger is causing stress or heightened interest.
- Regardless of whether your dog is nervous or frustrated, the strategy remains the same: move him to a new location to ease distress.

Chapter 6
STRESS LEVELS ASSESSMENT

🐾

We have limited ways of determining if a dog is calm or stressed. Since we can't ask our dogs if they are feeling okay, we have to rely on all the tools we have at our disposal. The clicker is the best and most consistent option for evaluating your dog's stress.

Your dog should be in front of you and closer to the trigger than you. AS SOON as your dog looks at the trigger or hears the trigger, 'click' and evaluate his reaction. This point bears repeating. When your dog looks **AT THE TRIGGER**, 'click' and treat.

The reason I repeated this is that you might have learned at some point to reward your dog when he looks at you. That is useful if you are working on eye contact during obedience practice, but that is not what I am referring to here. Asking or waiting for eye contact when a dog is stressed is a different strategy and I don't think it works as well.

**Your dog should be
closer to the other dog so
you can see everything
in front of you.**

You should mark the moment your dog experiences something, by 'clicking' with the clicker to check in with him. "Are you more concerned with what is in front of you, or do you want this tasty treat behind your head?"

ASSESSMENT OPPORTUNITIES

Learn to recognize your dog's response to the 'click' when working with a variety of triggers. For instance, when your dog sees his favorite playmate Fluffy walking by, he might not pay attention to the 'click' because his girlfriend distracted him. He isn't afraid, but just more interested in Fluffy than treats. By observing his behavior in a variety of situations, you can understand your dog's clicker responses and notice any shifts in his reactions. This awareness helps you make informed decisions about how your dog will react the next time he sees a trigger.

The following examples show common responses to the 'click' which correspond to the dog's emotional state. The goal is that your dog stays within the **CALM** zone. If your dog is in the **OVER THRESHOLD** zone, you should always move him away.

CALM
When he hears the 'click', he immediately turns away from the trigger, looks at you, and takes the treat gently.

DISTRACTED OR NERVOUS
He hesitates when he hears the 'click,' but turns around and takes the treat gently.

MORE DISTRACTED OR NERVOUS
He doesn't turn away from the trigger, but keeps his attention on it. When you reach forward with the treat, he takes it gently.

OVER THRESHOLD
- He doesn't take the treat.

- Barking, growling or lunging. Any obvious, over-excited or anxious response, including stiffness, hard stare, or heavy breathing.
- He takes the treat with a "rough mouth" and snatches it out of your hand and immediately looks back at the trigger.

DO NOT IGNORE A ROUGH MOUTH

Hopefully, your dog takes treats from your fingers gently and does not cause you discomfort. Pay attention to how she takes treats when she is completely calm, with no triggers present. That is her baseline. If that changes after you 'click' and she whips around, takes the treat roughly, "and gets back to business," that is a sign of stress and you should move her away. She wants the treat, but needs to focus her attention back on the trigger as soon as possible, resulting in a quick reaction and a painful experience for you.

ROUGHEST MOUTH EVER

In Chicago, I was working with a family that had a dog-aggressive dog, named Jake. The neighbor brought his dog, Wrigley, outside and we worked with him. At six feet apart, Jake seemed totally calm and under control. I took one step towards Wrigley and 'clicked' when Jake looked at him. Jake whipped his head around and took the treat so roughly that it felt like he was taking my fingers with him. I took one step farther back, 'clicked' and Jake took the treat as gently as any dog I have worked with.

Of course I had to try it again.

One stop forward, 'click' and immediately regretted it as pain shot through my hand due to the painful bite.

The points to remember are that subtle changes can make a huge difference and physiological responses to triggers are not random or intentional. When stressed, your dog reacts in a certain way. It is your responsibility to analyze your dog's reactions to the world around him and make adjustments to keep him and everyone else, safe and comfortable.

WHAT CAN YOU LEARN FROM YOUR DOG'S REACTION?

By using these evaluation strategies, you can determine your dog's limits and how they respond to different triggers. Can he be ten feet away from a dog, or does he need to be twenty feet? Is he as calm with a jogger as he is with someone simply walking by? Is he more comfortable with men or women? What is his response if a dog barks behind a fence? Can he remain calm in the same situation for five minutes, or does he get nervous after three minutes?

I like to think of the clicker as a tool to ask a dog: "Hey, what do you think about what you are currently experiencing?" You 'click' when he looks *at* the trigger **NOT** when he looks at you, or you 'click' when he hears a trigger, such as a barking dog or firetruck. You want him to see or hear the trigger and then you will evaluate what his instantaneous response is after he hears the 'click.'

Is he worried or interested in what he is looking at? In that case, his behavior will be like one of the **Nervous**, **More Nervous** or **Over Threshold** examples above. If he is completely calm around the trigger, he will turn away from the trigger to gently collect his tasty treat.

Keep your dog out of the **Over Threshold** zone as much as possible, but if your dog frequently moves in and out of the **Nervous** or **More Nervous** zones, then he might get more agitated. You will make much more progress if you keep your dog in the **Calm** zone.

If he is clicker-charged, you are using amazing treats, and he is not too interested in the trigger in front of him, he should turn towards you when you 'click.' It is that simple.

WHAT IF YOUR DOG STOPS TAKING TREATS?
If your dog just stops taking treats when on a walk. What do you do? It can happen when you take one step out of your home, or at any point during the walk.

"No thanks, I lost my appetite."

If your dog stops taking treats, stop using the clicker in that situation. The more frequently you 'click' and your dog refuses a treat, the more likely that he will ignore the clicker in all situations. Then, it is not a useful evaluation tool. If you decide to continue the walk, periodically offer your dog a treat without 'clicking.' If your dog takes treats again, it typically means that you can now start using the clicker and you will see a normal response.

KEEP TREATS INTERESTING

One important strategy is to rotate high value treats periodically to keep them interesting. One of my favorite foods is sushi, but if I ate it every day, I might get sick of it too. I suggest having three to five high-value treats that you only use when walking your dog. It keeps them fresh and interesting.

There have been MANY times that my client confidently proclaims that their dog is not treat motivated. I bring out the dried liver, chicken jerky, beef treats, or other high-value treats, and their dog usually becomes mesmerized and takes treats easily. A Rottweiler I worked with liked oyster crackers more than roast beef! Experiment with treats to find your dog's three to five favorites.

USE SQUEAKY OR TUG TOYS

Dogs will not play if they are under duress. If there's a threat present, their priorities shift to more important matters. If your dog typically enjoys toys, experiment with presenting a toy and playing with your dog after you 'click.'

You can assess her reaction by 'clicking' and waving a toy in front of her when she sees another dog. If she stops looking at the other dog and starts playing, that means she is comfortable. You are also creating a positive association around triggers. "When I see a dog, I get my favorite toy? Cool!"

SHOULD YOU BRING YOUR DOG HOME?

You should decide if your dog is completely over-threshold, stressed and needs a break. If your dog is too distracted or nervous and stops eating treats, you can sometimes still continue the walk without causing emotional harm.

Decide this on a case-by-case basis, but as long as there is enough space to stay clear of potential triggers, your dog is not exhibiting obvious stress signals such as barking, jerky head movements, a tucked tail, or heavy breathing then you can probably continue the walk.

SEE PROGRESS OVER TIME

If your dog stops taking treats in a certain location or after some time on a walk, hopefully you see he takes treats eventually in those situations. If you are actively working on lowering your dog's stress levels, then your dog should become more comfortable. When he takes treats, that is one sign he is calm. Be patient and continue to evaluate your dog's stress levels in all situations.

DOGS ARE A TRIGGER, BUT GARAGE DOORS?

Remember stacked and compound triggers? If your dog is noticeably nervous around dogs, he might also get nervous when a garage door opens, someone closes their car door, a firetruck rumbles by, or he hears kids playing in the playground. To ease triggers building up and putting your dog over his threshold, I suggest 'clicking' and treating whenever your dog notices a trigger outside. Once you identify your dog is comfortable near a trigger, you can 'click' and treat less frequently and eventually stop all together.

USE RECORDINGS TO DESENSITIZE TO NOISES

If you notice your dog reacting to noises outside, use recordings inside to desensitize him. You can control the volume so you are not putting your dog over his threshold. If he gets stressed multiple times on walks, the stress can build to a noticeable reaction. You can download the YouTube to MP3 program to your computer at www.4kdownload.com or simply record noises or use YouTube. You should play the audio files at a low volume on your phone or tablet and toss treats to your dog. As long as he easily takes the treat, the volume is not too loud. Eventually he will ignore those noises.

OVERALL STRESS REDUCTION

Every time your dog gets stressed, it is more likely he will get more stressed the next time he experiences that event. Notice everything that causes your dog discomfort and work on lowering his reaction around all of those triggers.

SUMMARY

- Observe your dog's reactions to triggers and use the clicker when he looks at or hears the trigger.
- Stacked and compound triggers can lead to pushing your dog past his comfort zone. If your dog stops taking treats, stop clicking in that situation, rotate high-value treats, and consider if your dog needs a break or a safer location.
- Use recordings to desensitize to noises.

Chapter 7
BODY LANGUAGE

Besides evaluating how your dog responds to the 'click' and the treat, you can learn a lot about your dog's stress levels by monitoring his body language. The clicker is one tool to assess how your dog responds to a situation, but there are a lot of body language cues if you know what to look for.

My dog, Sky, is wonderful, but he doesn't warm up to dogs or people immediately. However, he is very stable, easy to read, and fantastic to work with. I bring him to sessions frequently to work with my client's dogs.

If Sky is not interested in interacting with a dog or person, he maintains his distance or takes a step back if they come closer. We have a great working relationship and I do not put him in harm's way. He has learned that he can subtly tell me how he is feeling and I will keep him safe. If I wasn't paying attention or ignored his subtle signals, he might feel that he needs to growl or bark in order to make sure everyone is aware of his feelings.

NOTICE CHANGES IN YOUR DOG

Growling, barking and snarling are obvious signs of discomfort, but you need to learn about your dog's subtle signals. Every part of your dog's body can tell a story about how he is doing. Overall, you are looking for calm body language vs. tense, stiff, or quick changes in his posture or movements.

"I yawn every time
I see another dog."

HERE ARE SOME INDICATORS OF STRESS:

- **Yawning.** Dogs might yawn during or after a stressful event. Notice patterns of behavior. If a child runs by and your dog yawns, it might mean he is nervous around children.
- **Licking Lips.** If dogs are stressed, they might lick their lips. I notice this behavior more in small dogs. You should look for it as you are walking towards another dog as well as watch your dog for this behavior.
- **Shaking.** Dogs can shake as if they are wet and trying to dry themselves off. Sometimes an itchy collar or harness can cause a dog to shake, so you have to pay attention to patterns to determine if this is a signal to look out for.

- **Quick Movements.** It's best if a dog turns around right after the 'click', but a fast turn could indicate more tension than a slow, controlled one.
- **Jerky Movements.** Scanning, hunting and fast head movements when walking is not a good sign. A relaxed dog will ignore things happening around him.
- **Rough Mouth.** If your dog normally takes treats gently, move your dog away immediately if he takes them quickly and nips your fingers. This is absolutely a sign of stress.
- **Hard Stare.** If you see your dog or another dog fixated on something, that usually means they are uncomfortable and have to monitor the potential threat.
- **Closing Mouth.** If your dog looks at something and then clamps their mouth shut, this can be an indicator of stress.
- **Stiffness.** Stiffness can show up in any part of a dog's body, including shoulders, neck, eyes, mouth, wrinkled brow, or legs. Having "waxy" movements is a description of a dog walking with stiff legs.
- **Stalking.** Think of a cheetah stalking prey. This typically indicates stress. Some dogs will exhibit this behavior and then go into full play mode with their friends. You need to pay attention to your dog's body language to determine patterns.
- **Whites of a Dog's Eyes.** For dogs that don't have naturally droopy eyes (Bassets, Bloodhounds, St. Bernards), you might not see any white on the top,

bottom or sides when they are calm. If you see white, it usually means the dog is stressed. If you see white on the bottom of a dog's eyes, it can indicate that they are guarding something and have their mouth near the object with their eyes raised.

- **Quick Sideways Glances.** If a dog looks side to side as another dog is approaching, this indicates stress. I usually read it as the dog is looking for an escape route. You will often see white in the dog's eyes when they are doing this.

- **Hackles.** The hair on the back of a dog can stand up when they are aroused. Sometimes it means they are excited, but it usually means they are nervous.

- **Lowering Their Head.** If a dog is confident and not bothered by anything, they will usually stand tall, casually looking around. When a dog stares at something and lowers their head, it typically signifies uncertainty about what they are seeing. Assume this dog is anxious.

- **Bathroom Locations.** Often newly adopted dogs that are nervous do not feel comfortable urinating and defecating everywhere. This might have to do with not wanting to interfere with another dog's territory. This can manifest as a dog only eliminating near their home or backyard or not using those areas and only eliminating away from the home. As a dog becomes more confident, this will change.

- **Dilated Pupils.** If a dog's pupils enlarge (dilate), it is an sign that he is stressed, although it is difficult to see in most situations.
- **Sphinx Down.** If you are concerned that your dog is stressed and he is lying with his legs beneath him in a straight line, this can be a sign of stress. He is alert and more likely to jump up from this position vs. a down position with his legs on one side of his body.

NOTICE CHANGES IN OTHER DOGS

Understanding body language will help when you are approaching another dog to determine if the other dog is comfortable and safe to be around. Keep in mind that there are no guarantees. Some dogs can look very stable until they are within biting range and then bite without warning.

EARS — NOT MY FAVORITE INDICATOR

While many trainers point to a dog's ears to evaluate stress levels, I actually find they are the least useful indicator of stress. Ears can be back when a dog is blissfully happy or nervous. They can be erect if they are trying to make themselves bigger or simply if they are listening to something. I focus on other parts of a dog's body first.

Although individual ear movements may be difficult to interpret, I observe any ear movement to determine when a dog notices a trigger. Often ears "perk up" when they spot a new trigger. At that moment, I will 'click' and evaluate their response.

TAILS ARE USEFUL TO MONITOR STRESS

If your dog has a tail, you probably know your dog's "happy tail." Use that as a guide to compare it in other situations. Most dogs position their "happy tail" higher than their back and move it quickly back and forth. A "helicopter tail" is moving in a complete circle. I have never seen a dog exhibiting a helicopter tail that is anything but thrilled to be alive at that moment.

READING TAIL POSITIONS AND MOVEMENT

- **Lowered.** Even if a dog lowers their tail a few inches, this is a red flag that they are uncomfortable. They are afraid or submissive. Either way, you need to be more cautious that this dog might feel threatened.
- **Tucked.** If a dog puts its tail between its legs, that indicates stress.
- **Cat Tail.** When a dog with a long tail moves their tail from side to side, parallel to the ground and just moves the tip, this is usually a sign of concern or discomfort.

FLINCH? STRESS!

One really useful trick is to see if your dog flinches when you touch his back on a walk. The next time your dog is fixated on something, glide your finger along his spine. If he flinches or turns towards you quickly, that shows that he is nervous. He was focused on something that caught his attention and then you caught him by surprise, which made him jump.

"What was that?!"

As we have discussed, the buildup of stress throughout the walk can lead to stiffness and quick reactions. This is one way to gather more information about how your dog is doing before he surprises you with a lunge or a bark. If he flinches when you touch him, move him away from what he is looking at and work at a farther distance.

POSITIVE INDICATORS

There are indicators that predict that a dog is comfortable. While a dog can be comfortable in one instance, a slight change in the environment can cause stress and reactivity. It is important that you monitor your dog frequently to avoid surprises.

- **Flag Tail.** If a dog moves his tail high in the air and waves the tip, it usually means that he is confident and happy. When he dog enters a dog park, he might do this as a sign to the other dogs that he is friendly. After a quick sniff, often there will be a play bow and play will start.

- **Play Bow.** A dog is being friendly if he crouches down and puts his tail up in the air.
- **Looking at the Person.** If your dog is comfortable around people and ignores a dog, this is a good sign that the other dog is not a threat.
- **Sitting or Lying Down.** If your dog sits or lies down on his own (without you asking) it means that he is more comfortable than if he were intently focused on the other dog while standing stiffly.
- **Able to Perform Obedience.** If you think your dog is comfortable, ask for a behavior that he can usually perform flawlessly. If he can do that behavior without hesitation, it means he is comfortable.
- **Bouncy Movements.** This is the opposite of stiff, waxy movements. If two dogs are interacting and bouncing around, it means they are comfortable.
- **Able to Play With Toys.** Dogs that are anxious won't take treats or play with toys. If your dog sees another dog and then plays with a toy, he is not anxious.
- **Continuous, Comfortable Movements.** This is the opposite of stiffness. A dog is at ease when his mouth is open, eyes relaxed, tail wagging, and he scans the surroundings. If that changes and he stops moving a part of his body, observe what he noticed that caused a stressful response.

SUMMARY

- You can gauge your dog's stress levels by observing their body language in addition to their response to training cues.

- Pay attention to your dog's reactions to other dogs and people. If your dog maintains distance or steps back, it may indicate discomfort.

- Look for subtle signals of stress in your dog's body language, such as yawning, lip licking, shaking, quick or jerky movements, a hard stare, or a closed mouth.

- Understanding body language is essential when approaching other dogs to assess their comfort and safety.

- The position and movement of a dog's tail can provide valuable insights into their emotional state, including lowered, tucked, or "cat tail" positions indicating stress, and a high, wagging tail indicating confidence and happiness.

Chapter 8
KNOW YOUR DOG

There are two categories of leash reactivity. It's useful to determine whether a dog is fearful or socially awkward, even though they are treated similarly.

FEARFUL DOGS

Dogs that are fearful want another dog to move away from them. They are communicating through body movements and vocalization, "Get away!" But, if they aren't successful in getting the other dog to move away, they get more afraid and their behaviors become more pronounced.

FRUSTRATED OR SOCIALLY AWKWARD DOGS

Dogs that are not afraid of other dogs but do not act appropriately when interacting with other dogs can be called *Socially Awkward*. They can also exhibit reactivity when barriers such as a fence, leash, or window stop them from interacting with other dogs. The frustration and inappropriate behaviors can build to a point that it can cause aggression, even if a dog's intentions start out friendly. If a dog *wants* to interact with another dog; it doesn't mean they can remain calm as the other dog moves closer, if there is any physical contact or even if the other dog simply glances at them.

Your dog might want to say "hello," but he might not know how to act once the other dog gets closer. Reactions can include submissive behavior or aggressive actions like barking, growling, snapping, or biting. It is embedded in a dog's DNA to be social. They want to be near other dogs or people, but things can go badly if something happens that they are not prepared for.

"Um, Hi."

IT TAKES TWO TO TANGO

If your dog approaches another dog too quickly, the other dog can get defensive and attack him. This experience can cause emotional damage and your dog can become fearful around other dogs. Your dog should always be as calm as possible when approaching other dogs. Use the movement strategies and **Four-Step Greetings** strategies explained later in this book to help calm your overexcited dog.

QUESTIONS TO ASK

If your dog is reactive because of fear or is socially awkward and frustrated, the strategies are similar, but knowing the intensity and history of the reactivity is important for safety. Dogs that are frustrated or socially awkward might calm down when allowed to get closer to other dogs. Dogs that are fearful are usually reactive at any distance.

1. Does your dog have any friends that they can interact with or play with?

If your dog has has dog friends that they can interact with, it typically means that his reactivity stems from frustration.

2. Can your dog play off leash safely?

If your dog can play off leash appropriately with other dogs, but shows reactivity when on leash, then frustration is the root cause of the reactivity.

3. Has your dog snapped at or bitten another dog?

If this has occurred, it means that you need to be extremely careful when interacting with another dog. A muzzle might be necessary, and proper management and distance is always critically important.

4. How far away is your dog before he or she reacts?

Some dogs can be very close to other dogs or even sniff before an aggressive reaction occurs. Other dogs bark wildly when a dog is thirty feet away or more. Being cautious is key in both cases, so make sure to practice movement and desensitization strategies at a safe distance when introducing two dogs.

5. What does the reaction look like?

Frustration – If a dog exhibits whining, random play bows, interspersed with barking, this means a dog is frustrated and socially awkward. They want to be closer to the other dog, but are in turmoil. They don't feel confident being patient and quiet. They *want* to be closer to the other dog, but sometimes react aggressively when a dog exhibits a behavior that they are not expecting. Sometimes a dog that performs these contradictory behaviors can play beautifully off leash but becomes frustrated and inconsistent when on a leash.

Fear – If a dog consistently barks intensely possibly with low guttural growls or snarling, this behavior shows a dog who is fearful.

Some fear aggressive dogs can peacefully interact with other dogs that they live with or have known since they were much younger. Be cautious around new dogs.

Aggressive tendencies may result from unpleasant experiences with dogs or lack of proper socialization. If your dog has fear aggression, you have to be more careful since there isn't a history of safe, pleasant experiences with dogs. With a fear aggressive dog, you need to first work on his fear and then work on social skills through measured, repeated exposure.

WHAT SHOULD YOU DO WITH THIS INFORMATION?
The desensitization and movement exercises can help lower reactivity whether the root cause is fear or frustration. If your dog can safely play with other dogs, you can use walks, play sessions, or the dog park to help them socialize and minimize frustration when on leash.

If your dog is highly reactive, has an unknown history, does not show warning signals, has bitten another dog, or behaves unpredictably, use caution and practice the desensitization and movement strategies. You should also consider using a muzzle when near other dogs or people.

GOAL VS. REALITY
Some dogs simply can't play with other dogs or get close to them. You may need to adjust your expectations based on your dog's behavior. At the very least, I want you to have more enjoyable walks with your dog.

He might never enter dog parks, play with other dogs, be boarded with other dogs, or be trusted with other dogs. You need to adjust your expectations based on daily practice at a safe, controlled distance. If he has injured dogs, bitten without warning or has been inconsistent in his reactivity, he should not be close to other dogs, and you should consider using a muzzle. Seek immediate help from your veterinarian to discuss anti-anxiety medication and also enlist the help of a skilled positive reinforcement dog trainer.

NEW DOG? ASSUME THE WORST

If you adopted a dog recently and do not know his history, you need to be extremely cautious and assume that he can't safely interact with other dogs or people. I follow the rule of "assume the worst and hope for the best" with dog behavior. Take your time and get to know your dog before allowing close interactions with other dogs or people. Always have your dog on a leash in new situations.

Is this my new home?

I have been burned firsthand with a brand new dog. In Chicago, I was walking with my two Collies and my Sheltie. I saw a Labrador Retriever walking by that I had never seen. I asked his owner if he was friendly. He was calm and seemed friendly. She replied, "Oh yes, he is friendly!"

I let my dogs say, "Hello" and the other dog immediately attacked one of my Collies, resulting in a mouthful of my dog's fur in his mouth. The dog's owner informed me she was sorry, but she just adopted him yesterday. In other words, she did not know her dog!

CONTINUE OFF LEASH PLAY?
Some dogs can play beautifully off leash but become extremely aggressive when you put them on leash. If you are sure that your dog is always safe and appropriate off leash, then you can continue allowing this.

However, there are situations where things can become dangerous even when a dog is off leash. If you attempt to control your dog during a park fight by grabbing his collar or harness, he may become aggressive towards you or a nearby dog or person. It also can be challenging removing your dog from the play area without putting him on leash. If you put the leash on and other dogs come too close, he can become aggressive.

OFF-LEASH PLAY CREATING ON-LEASH PROBLEMS
Dogs that routinely visit daycare and dog parks can become leash aggressive when they see other dogs while they are on leash. This can occur even if they play beautifully off leash. If they are used to seeing dogs and immediately playing with them, they can become frustrated if they cannot play with every dog they see. Leash aggression is more likely to happen if they also bark out of windows or behind a fence repeatedly throughout the day.

For dogs that can safely be off leash but are aggressive on leash, the best thing to do is to work on reducing the on-leash aggression as much as possible so it diminishes or goes away entirely. You can use regular parks and trails to exercise your dog on a leash and work on strategies to reduce frustration. Also see the **Dog Park Section** to learn how to use a dog park to fix this problem.

THE DANGERS OF RESOURCE GUARDING

Resource Guarding is another cause of reactivity. Resource guarding is the action of guarding or protecting resources, including tennis balls, bones, toys, or locations such as a dog bed, a food bowl, or a crate. Dogs can also guard people. This book does not cover toy guarding or dog park aggression, but the same rules apply to dogs being aggressive because of guarding, or because of wariness of others being too close. You should evaluate your dog and other dog's stress levels and keep him at a distance where both dogs are calm.

Dogs that guard tennis balls or other objects should not be in dog parks where it is impossible to control access to toys. In that case, your dog should only play with other dogs in small play groups where you can ensure that those objects will not be present.

SUMMARY
- The two main reasons for on-leash reactivity in dogs are fear and frustration.

- Fearful dogs want other dogs to move away from them, while frustrated dogs want to interact with other dogs, but barriers like a leash, window, or fence prevent them from doing so.
- Dogs may display awkward behavior when they want to interact with other dogs but don't know how to behave properly, resulting in unpredictable reactions like barking, growling, snapping, or biting.
- Socially awkward dogs can provoke aggression in other dogs because of their excessive behavior.
- Resource guarding can lead to reactivity and aggression, so it requires careful management to keep each dog calm and prevent aggressive responses.

Chapter 9
DON'T IGNORE BEHAVIORS

🐾

If your dog repeatedly reacts a certain way, this behavior will take more time to change or it might never change. In addition, if your dog barks or gets agitated when he sees other dogs, his frustration will increase.

Besides increased frustration and reactivity, dogs can think that their barking is "working" because the dog or other trigger moves away when they bark. "Wow! All I have to do is bark and the dog will move away from me!"

Whether the initial response is because of fear or frustration, the trigger moving away reinforces the dog's barking. Your dog doesn't realize the dog would have moved away no matter what. He can think his barking worked, so he repeats the behavior every time he sees a dog. Unfortunately, dogs don't "outgrow" these undesirable behavior patterns. Your dog's barking may continue unless you decrease their stress levels.

Several years ago, my client's two dogs would bark every morning in the backyard while she had coffee and got ready for work, which annoyed her. I explained to her that if she allows her dogs to bark each morning, this behavior will never change. Either she should desensitize them to the triggers by being in the yard and working with them, or she should bring them inside. It disappointed her that there wasn't a quick fix to the problem, but she understood that it takes time. She sent me an email a few weeks later thanking me for the suggestions and reported back that her situation was much better.

FENCE RUNNING IS NOT GOOD

Most people do not appreciate the barking and dead grass that results from their dog "playing" with the neighbor's dog by running back and forth and barking along the fence line. However, at least they are getting tired, right? Well, no. Most likely your dog is getting over-stimulated, frustrated and potentially aggressive. It is never a good idea to let behaviors stemming from anxiety to run their course. It rarely ends well.

HOW TO FIX WINDOW OR FENCE REACTIVITY

While the focus of this book is leash aggression, it is important to note the significant role that repeated barking plays in this problem. Each time your dog gets agitated, frustration and reactivity increase which makes treatment more difficult.

As described previously, use the clicker to desensitize your dog to triggers. Make sure your dog is on a leash so you can move him away if needed. Whether your dog is inside your home near the window or in the backyard, 'click' as soon as he turns towards a trigger. If he doesn't respond immediately to the 'click' or if he barks or other undesired behavior, gently move him away until he stops barking or turns away from the trigger.

When inside, one easy strategy is 'click' and toss a treat on your dog's back every time he walks towards the window. If he is more interested in what is outside and ignores the tasty treat, you should gently grab the leash and move him away because he is most likely going to bark.

I'M NEAR THE WINDOW . . . WHERE'S MY TREAT?

Eventually your dog will anticipate getting a treat near the window and his focus will change from hunting for things to bark at outside and instead will look for treats on the floor and he will be more calm.

Working in the backyard looks the same as all the other outdoor exercises in this book. If your dog cannot be calm when he looks at your neighbor or another trigger, move him to a different location until he calms down, or take him inside.

As you work more with him in the backyard or behind a window, you can pick your triggers based on the intensity of your dog's response. You can keep using the clicker when your dog sees the mailman, but use it less often for joggers.

"Good job! Isn't it fun when joggers run by? You are doing so well! What a good dog!"

If you can distract him only with your voice, it means that he isn't very interested in the trigger and he is getting desensitized. I will explain this strategy more later in this book.

If you can't work with your dog when you are both inside, try keeping him with you or using barriers like window shades, opaque window film, baby gates, or a crate to prevent him from looking out the window or barking. Make sure to always be with your dog outside as well until this problem is fixed. You are not doing him any favors by letting him "talk" to the neighbors all day long. He is simply getting more stressed and his reactivity will increase.

SUMMARY

- Repeatedly rehearsing a behavior makes it more difficult to change.
- Dogs don't naturally "outgrow" undesirable behaviors; modification is necessary.
- Desensitization and management techniques can improve your dog's response to triggers at home, in the yard, or on leash.
- 'Click' as soon as your dog sees a trigger and evaluate his response. If he doesn't turn around immediately towards the 'click,' gently move him away and work at a farther distance.

Chapter 10
LEASH HANDLING STRATEGIES

It can be overwhelming trying to incorporate these new strategies you are learning. The more you practice, the more comfortable you will feel and it will eventually be second-nature. Understanding how to hold the leash, clicker, and treats properly can make your training session more productive.

The leash is used to control your dog and prevent her from running into the street or getting too close to other people or dogs. With this in mind, it is extremely important that you are always aware of how you are holding the leash. If you only use one hand, you will not have the level of control that is necessary to be as safe and in control as possible.

For the most control, loop one hand through the end of the leash and the other hand should hold the leash closer to your dog. If your dog is agitated and pulling towards a dog or a person, use your hand positioned on the leash to gently guide her farther away. This hand acts as your steering and brake.

The leash you use should feel comfortable and not too thick for your hands. I provide leash recommendations at the end of the book. I want you to practice holding the leash when it is not attached to your dog, regardless of the leash you are currently using.

I do not recommend using a retractable leash. That type of leash limits your ability to maintain control of your dog.

Here are the instructions for holding the clicker and the leash. You should use a treat pouch for easier access to treats and also to free up one of your hands.

LEASH HANDLING STRATEGIES

1. Loop the leash around your wrist.
2. Grab the hanging leash with your other hand and loop it around one finger.
3. Turn your hand over so you can grip the leash.
4. Put the clicker in the same hand.
5. Either put treats in the same hand or use a treat pouch to hold the treats.
6. The other hand should always be empty and ready to hold the leash to act as your steering and brake for more control.
7. The leash should be loose as much as possible. A tight leash will create more stress and reactivity.

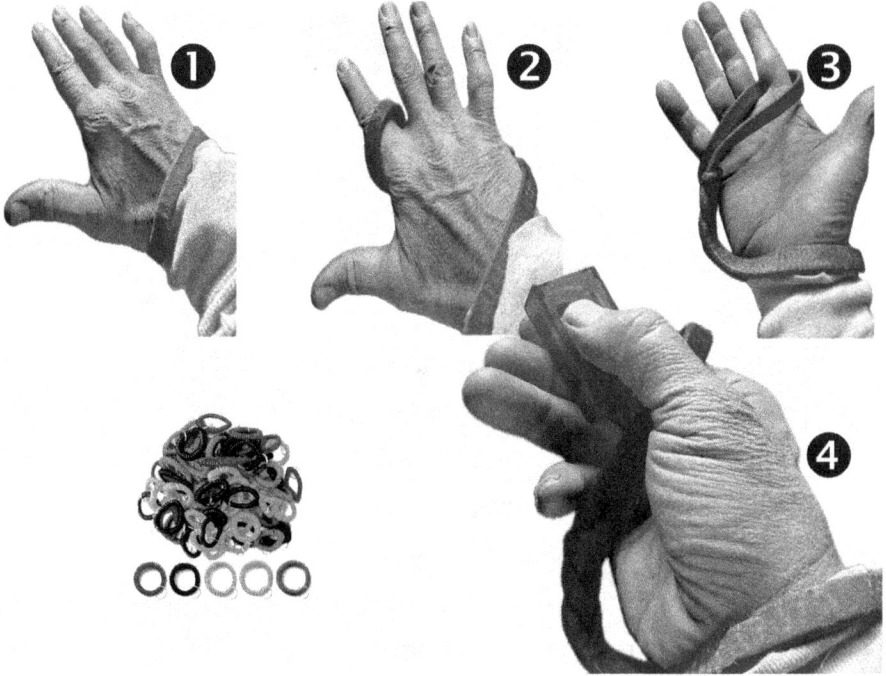

Note: Leash handling is so much easier if you use a stretchy wrist keychain to hold the clicker. You can find these on Amazon, hardware stores, gas stations or other locations. An example is shown above.

Chapter 11
POSITIONING AND ANALYSIS

Dogs react out of fear or frustration. Your dog feels afraid or uncomfortable around the other dog or person, or she experiences frustration because she cannot get closer. Your dog's agitated behavior might cause another dog to react even if your dog's intention was to play with the other dog.

A trigger is anything your dog notices which causes a behavior change. If you want to change your dog's response to a trigger, pay attention to two things:

1.   Your dog's position in relation to the trigger.
2.   Your dog's reaction to the trigger.

These are factual details that you can analyze. As an example, you could observe:

- **Your dog's position**: Your dog is ten feet away from another dog.
- **Your dog's reaction**: His eyes got bigger, his body got stiff, he started breathing faster, and then barked at the other dog.

What is the most effective strategy when working with your dog? It is very simple, **lower your dog's stress.** Stress leads to changes in your dog that then cause body stiffness, faster movements, and less tolerance for changes around him. This type of cycle leads to a *frustrated, reactive dog.* The more frequently a dog is exposed to the same trigger, the more agitated it becomes. This makes treatment more difficult.

POSITIONING IS IMPORTANT

It is important that you are in the correct position when your dog sees another dog. Make sure you can see your dog and the other dog at the same time. You are the farthest away from the other dog with your dog in front of you.

Your dog should be closer to the other dog so you can see everything in front of you.

YOUR DOG SHOULD BE CLOSER TO THE OTHER DOG

There are many reasons for the effectiveness of this strategy.

1. Everything is in front of you so you can observe and adjust your dog's distance from the trigger.

2. Your dog can trip you if he lunges towards the other dog while crossing in front of you.

3. You can see immediately when your dog is comfortable if he turns away from the other dog and towards you when he hears the 'click' or "yes!"

DON'T DO THIS

Many trainers recommend blocking your dog by standing between your dog and the other dog.

No. Don't do this. Everything is in *front* of you.

Do not block your dog.
If he is anxious, MOVE!

LOOSE LEASH IS KEY

One important point to keep in mind with on-leash aggression, is that a tight leash increases a dog's stress. It prevents free movement and limits their options. Dogs also look more aggressive to the other dog since their body is stiff, which can signify being worried and potentially aggressive. Having dogs meet head-on is counter-productive, and in the following pages, I will show you strategies to avoid a tight leash. Tight leash = more stress.

INSIDE PRACTICE EXERCISE

I want you to first practice your positioning inside. Have someone help you and ask them to sit or stand in one location. Put your dog on a leash and position him closer to your helper in a direct line so your dog and your helper are in front of you with your dog between the two of you. Have your dog as far away from your helper as possible.

The goal of this is to observe the ideal reaction when your dog sees a trigger and then hears the 'click' of the clicker.

Your setup should look like this > You -- your dog -- helper. Your dog is in between you and your helper.

1. Have your helper tap his or her foot on the floor or tap on a piece of furniture gently. AS SOON as your dog looks towards the noise, 'click' or say, "YES!"
2. If your dog turns and faces you and takes the treat gently, the tapping noise did not bother him.
3. If your dog doesn't turn around immediately or doesn't take the treat gently, you can tell that he is distracted (excited) or nervous. Observe your dog's behavior to determine if he is too focused on the trigger.
4. If your dog does not turn around immediately, move farther away or have your helper tap more quietly. Find

an intensity where your dog turns around immediately when hearing the 'click.'

5. If your dog doesn't turn towards the 'click.' Try more interesting treats. That can help.

Your Helper

Your Dog

You

> 'Click' as soon as your dog looks at your helper. If he immediately turns towards you, he is more interested in the treat. That is your goal.

I want you to remember what it looked like when your dog turned around immediately after hearing the 'click.' That is what you want to see when you work with other triggers such as dogs or people outside. It means that he is not bothered by the trigger, it means that he is not frustrated. It means that he is getting desensitized to the motion or sound. That is the goal!

SUMMARY

- On-leash aggression in dogs is a reaction to a trigger, often stemming from fear or frustration.
- Practice positioning inside with a helper and your dog on a leash, with the dog between you and the helper.
- To manage on-leash aggression, keep the leash loose, stay where you can see both your dog and the trigger, and don't stand between them.
- If your dog turns away from the trigger and takes the treat gently, they are not concerned about the trigger and your dog is getting desensitized.

Chapter 12
WORK OUTSIDE

It is useful to understand your dog's baseline mental state. As soon as you walk outside, before your dog sees another dog, 'click' and observe how your dog reacts in a calm state.

The valuable information includes:
- How does your dog respond to the 'click?'
  - Does he turn around immediately?
  - Does he remain turned towards you, or does he immediately start scanning the environment for triggers?
- Does he eat the treat?
  - Does he take the treat out of your hands with a rougher mouth than normal?
- How smooth or jerky are his movements?
  - Does he casually turn towards you, or does he seem stiff and on guard?

Once you have a baseline, compare your dog's behavior patterns after you 'click' when he sees a dog. Some dogs stop taking treats immediately when outside. Without a baseline study, you might mistake your dog's nervousness towards the new dog as the cause, when in reality, he was already nervous from the moment he stepped outside or doesn't like the treats.

If that happens, take some time and work more on outside desensitization work without dogs present. Your dog has generalized his anxiety to simply being outside. You should also experiment with different treats. Your dog might be bored with the current selection of treats.

WORK WITH DOGS
Now let's work on desensitizing your dog to another dog. Either enlist the help of a friend to bring their dog to work with you, or practice this strategy at a park or in your neighborhood. Start at a safe distance away from another dog, or position yourself in a well-trafficked area with dogs walking by. Start at least twenty to thirty feet away from other dogs. For reference, side streets in many neighborhoods are approximately thirty feet wide. Stand with your dog in front of you. AS SOON as your dog sees another dog, 'click' and attempt to give a treat.

What happened? Did your dog turn around towards you? Did he ignore the 'click' and bark at the other dog?

FIND THE CORRECT DISTANCE
The following illustration shows the ideal scenario. You are proactively working in a park or near a path with a lot of space and have found a distance where your dog is calm as he looks at other dogs walking by. This shows one dog moving from left

to right with his person working behind him. She should 'click' and treat each time her dog looks at the other dog. If he turns around immediately after hearing the 'click,' this is a success. As the other dog walks by, she should rotate her body so her dog is always in between her and the other dog. With each successful 'click' and treat, she can take one step closer to the path and continue working.

Positioning

Position yourself so your dog is between you and the other dog. 'Click' as soon as your dog sees him. Rotate your body as he walks by and 'click' each time your dog looks at him.

If you stay far enough away and 'click' and treat each time your dog sees another dog, you will accomplish two things:

1. Your dog is learning to see other dogs and not react.

2. You are learning the correct distance for your dog to remain calm.

Pay attention to this distance and start there the next time you work in this location and slowly move closer each time your dog turns towards you after the 'click.' With practice, you should be able to decrease the distance needed for your dog to remain calm.

STOPS RESPONDING TO THE 'CLICK' - MOVE
If your dog does not immediately turn around towards you after hearing the 'click,' gently lead him away as quickly as you can. Pulling him back on the leash restricts your dog's movements and can also make him appear aggressive to other dogs.

Lead him away by picking a safe direction to travel away from the other dog in the relative direction that your dog is facing. If the only safe option is to pull your dog away, do so, but whenever possible, lead, don't pull.

ONLY TWO OPTIONS
Whenever you are with your dog and he sees another dog, there are only two options:

1. Allow your dog to stay where he is.
2. Move your dog to another location.

If your dog gets agitated and stops responding to the 'click,' your only option is to move him to a new location. The next illustration explains that step.

USE THE "Y" OR "T" PATTERN IF YOUR DOG ISN'T CALM
You only need to use the "Y" or "T" strategy to move your dog to a farther location if your dog reacts aggressively, doesn't take the treat, or takes the treat roughly.

MOVE ONLY IF THE CLICKER ISN'T "WORKING"
When you move your dog, you are simply finding a location where your dog can be calm. If your dog is calm, as dogs are walking by or walking towards you, you don't need to move her. The goal is to remove her once she starts getting nervous, or even before, to prevent high stress levels.

The following image shows the starting point for you and your dog. The arrow pointing down shows the direction you would take if you pulled your dog back (not recommended). You are still moving your dog away, but your dog will most likely continue to look at the other dog. The leash will be tight, and it will take more time to get away.

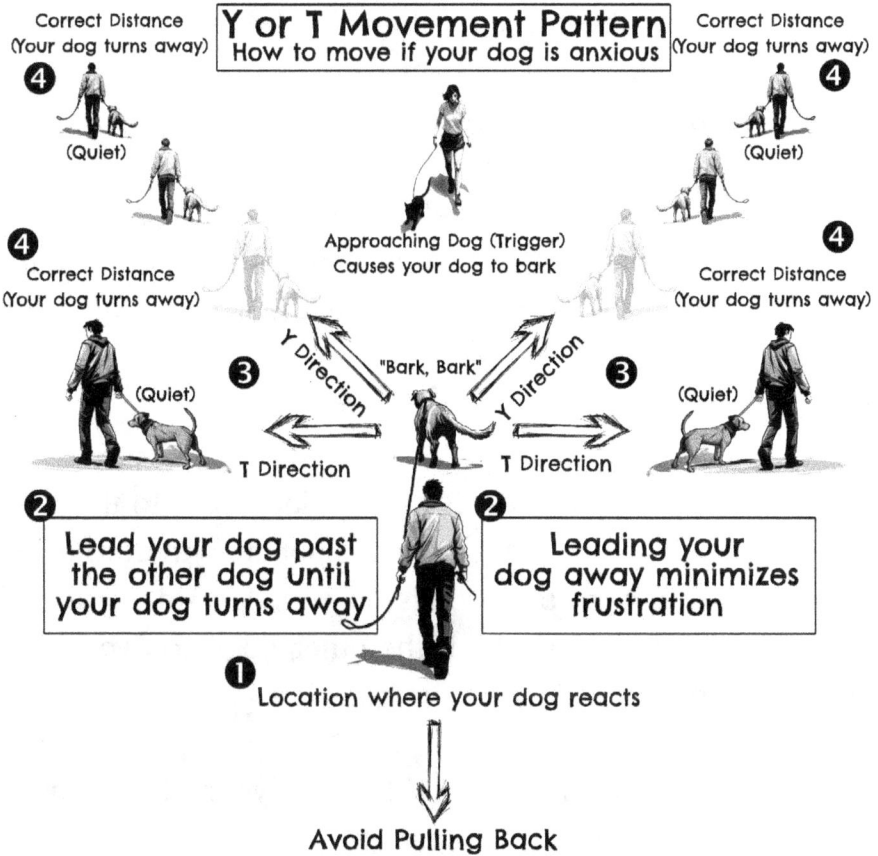

Correct Distance
(Your dog turns away)
4
(Quiet)

Y or T Movement Pattern
How to move if your dog is anxious

Correct Distance
(Your dog turns away)
4
(Quiet)

4
Correct Distance
(Your dog turns away)

Approaching Dog (Trigger)
Causes your dog to bark

Correct Distance
(Your dog turns away)
4

3
Y Direction
"Bark, Bark"
Y Direction
3
(Quiet)

(Quiet)
T Direction
T Direction

2
Lead your dog past the other dog until your dog turns away

2
Leading your dog away minimizes frustration

1
Location where your dog reacts

Avoid Pulling Back

TRAIN YOURSELF TO MOVE FORWARD
It is human nature to pull your dog back if there is a threat. I think everyone wants to keep the threat in front of them so they can continue evaluating the situation. If you can train

yourself to move forward and pass by the other dog, your dog will be more calm. This is only possible if there is enough space to do so safely. If you can only pull your dog backwards, do so, but find another area to practice in the future.

The other arrows show the recommended direction in the "Y" or "T" direction. Go left or right depending on which option gives you more space to safely move. You are moving away, but you are in front of your dog with your dog behind you and you are moving as quickly and safely as possible. You should keep moving until your dog looks away from the other dog. That is called a **demeanor shift** and indicates that your dog is not interested in the other dog at that distance. Movement is a natural option for a dog if they are under duress.

NOTE: Make sure your dog is on the side closer to the other dog when you are moving so she does not cross in front of you and trip you. If the other dog is on your left side, your dog should be on your left side. If the other dog is on your right side, your dog should be on your right side.

There are two main reasons leading your dog away is preferable to pulling your dog back from the other dog.

1. Leading your dog away is the fastest option to get your dog away from the stressful location and to a neutral location where you can continue working. Pulling back

on the leash results in more of a struggle for you since your dog is still pulling towards the other dog.

2. Leading your dog away reduces the time that there is a tight leash. A tight leash causes more stress with the dog being pulled away, and often causes the other dog to act negatively as well. A tight leash makes a dog look stiff. Stiffness is a sign of aggression. If there is a tight leash, your dog can look aggressive to the other dog, causing the whole scenario to escalate. Lead your dog away keeping tension on the leash only until your dog follows you and then release pressure on the leash.

HOW DO YOU KNOW HOW FAR TO MOVE YOUR DOG?

As soon as your dog stops paying attention to the other dog and turns away, it means your dog is less concerned with the other dog and he is more calm. This is called a *demeanor shift* and at this point, you have two options:

Option 1. As shown in the following illustration, stop walking and position yourself with your dog in front of you, with you looking directly at your dog's head. AS SOON as your dog looks at the other dog, 'click' and offer a treat.

At this point, the clicker might "work" and he will start paying attention to it again and take treats. As long as your dog is calm, you are achieving your goal.

Positioning

Position yourself so your dog is between you and the other dog. 'Click' as soon as your dog sees him. Rotate your body as he walks by and 'click' each time your dog looks at him.

Option 2. As shown in the following illustration, move towards the other dog and safely move past the other dog for another "pass" until he turns away again.

If you act quickly and immediately lead your dog away when your dog reacts, your dog is spending less time in an agitated state. You should lead your dog away as soon as he becomes agitated. Period.

Y or T Movement Pattern
How to move if your dog is anxious

Correct Distance
(Your dog turns away)
(Quiet)

Correct Distance
(Your dog turns away)
(Quiet)

Approaching Dog (Trigger)
Causes your dog to bark

Correct Distance
(Your dog turns away)

Correct Distance
(Your dog turns away)

Y Direction "Bark, Bark" Y Direction

(Quiet) (Quiet)

T Direction　　T Direction

Lead your dog past the other dog until your dog turns away

Leading your dog away minimizes frustration

Location where your dog reacts

Avoid Pulling Back

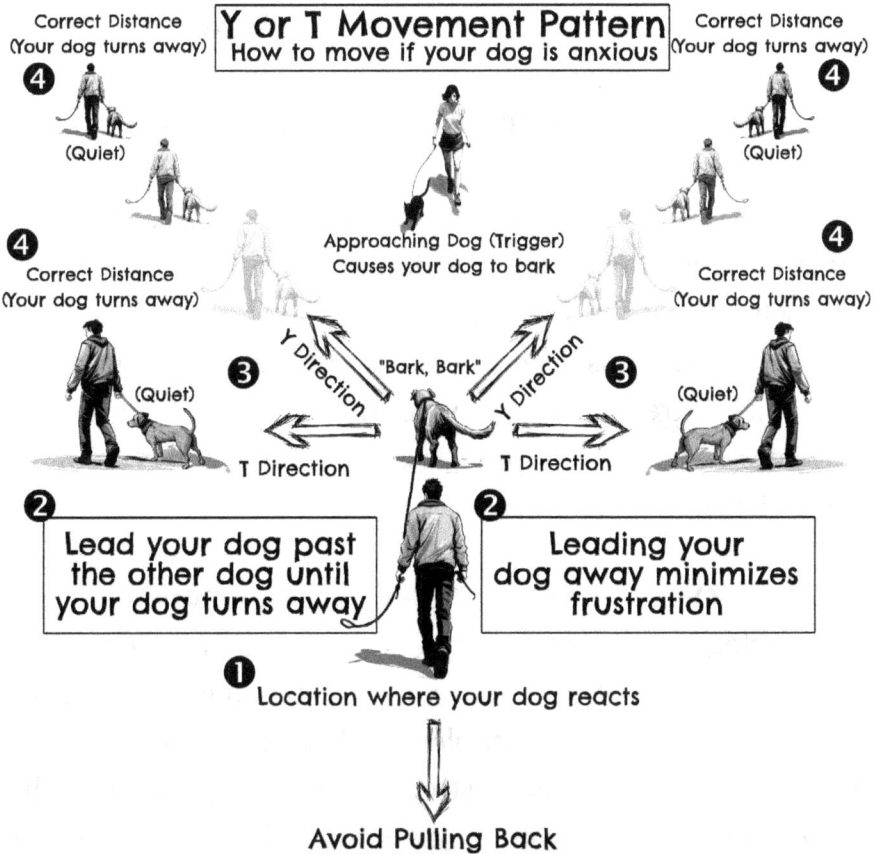

STOP USING THE CLICKER AND KEEP MOVING

If your dog is highly agitated and does not respond to the clicker and treats, you should take a break from using the clicker. Every time you 'click' and your dog ignores it, you are potentially desensitizing your dog to the clicker. At that point, the clicker loses its effectiveness. If you have enough space, simply move your dog back and forth at a safe distance from the other dog and watch his body language. If you are making progress, you will see a demeanor shift where your dog looks away from the other dog. As you pass back and forth, the demeanor shift might occur sooner after each pass. If your dog is getting more agitated, move farther away and try again.

If your dog isn't reacting to the clicker but still takes treats, you can remain in your current position unless they lunge or bark intensely. If that occurs, it means that your dog's stress levels are high, and he is over-threshold. Sudden movements also signal high stress levels. If your dog exhibits unpredictable movements, be more cautious. As soon as he stops responding to the clicker, move him away.

WHEN SHOULD YOU USE THE CLICKER AGAIN?

If your dog stops responding to the clicker and stops taking treats, stop using it. You can continue working with your dog as long as he is not completely shut down or noticeably agitated and getting more stressed. At that point, take him away from that location or go home. If you can continue working with your dog, occasionally offer him a treat without 'clicking.' When he takes treats again, this means he is calmer, and you can start using the clicker again.

SOMETIMES LOTS OF "LAPS" ARE NEEDED

Several years ago, I brought my dog, Sky, to a session with a client. She hired me because her dog was aggressive towards other dogs and she couldn't walk him without him barking and acting aggressively. She stopped taking her dog on walks because it was too stressful.

I had her walk Sky on a leash while I worked with her dog. As soon as her dog starting barking, I moved quickly back and forth in the "T" pattern. I moved back and forth twelve times. Her dog was barking repeatedly, but you know what happened? With each pass, her dog turned away from Sky sooner. At the beginning, I had to move past Sky about twenty feet before her dog stopped barking and lost interest.

With each pass back and forth, the demeanor shift happened sooner. After twelve passes, I stopped moving and spoke with my client less than five feet away and her dog was quiet. My client was shocked and so happy she started crying. In the three years that she had her dog, she said her dog was never this calm around another dog and she now had hope she could continue making progress.

AVOIDING ALL DOGS IS NOT THE ANSWER
Before clients hire me, many avoid all dogs on walks. They are often amazed and delighted to see me "hunting" for dogs and when I get really excited when the next dog approaches. One more opportunity to work on desensitization! They are sometimes nervous as I say, "Watch this!" and hurry towards another dog, but then they see the results and gain confidence.

Avoiding dogs increases frustration and prevents your dog from learning to be calm around other dogs. Part of your dog's doggy brain wants so badly to interact with that other dog. If you always go the other direction, her frustration goes up and her social skills go down. You can end up with an extremely frustrated, socially awkward dog that simply can't act in a calm, appropriate manner.

Multiple Passes To Lower Reactivity

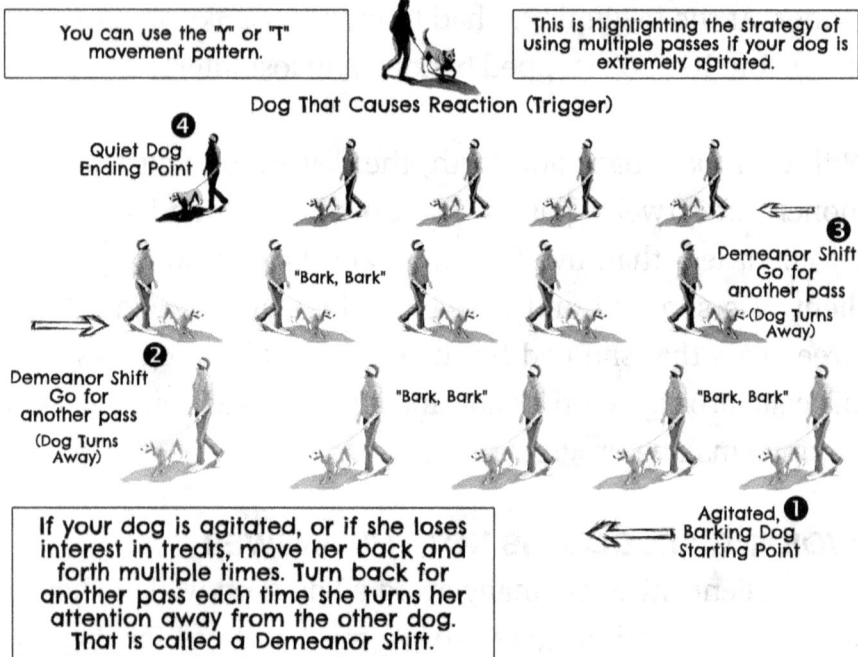

You can use the "Y" or "T" movement pattern.

This is highlighting the strategy of using multiple passes if your dog is extremely agitated.

Dog That Causes Reaction (Trigger)

4 Quiet Dog Ending Point

"Bark, Bark"

3 Demeanor Shift Go for another pass (Dog Turns Away)

2 Demeanor Shift Go for another pass (Dog Turns Away)

"Bark, Bark"

"Bark, Bark"

If your dog is agitated, or if she loses interest in treats, move her back and forth multiple times. Turn back for another pass each time she turns her attention away from the other dog. That is called a Demeanor Shift.

1 Agitated, Barking Dog Starting Point

REASONS MOVEMENT WORKS

I have practiced the movement strategies as described above thousands of times and found them to be extremely effective.

Here is why:

1. By immediately leading your dog away from triggers, they will be less stressed.
2. Movement is one natural defense response when a dog is under duress. If you force him to stay close to the

trigger that is causing him stress, he will get more stressed, not less. It will force him to be more obvious in his signals, such as growling or barking or biting. Get him out of there so he can calm down.

3. A tight leash is counter-productive. If a leash is tight because your dog is lunging towards a trigger or trying to get away, that will increase his anxiety since he can't get away.

4. A tight leash also makes a dog look more aggressive to the other dog. If your dog lunges at another dog, it can cause both dogs to become more stressed and react aggressively.

5. Movement also requires your dog to exert energy, and exercise is a natural way to reduce stress.

6. Frustration is a common reason dogs react on a leash. If you move your dog laterally at a safe distance from the other dog, your dog can say "Hello" to the other dog in a safe, measured way.

WHAT DOESN'T WORK

Before my clients hire me, they have often tried various strategies that did not work for them, whether their dog barks at dogs or people. Here are some examples.

- Avoiding all dogs. Walking in the other direction as soon as your dog sees another dog or your dog barks.
  - **Why this doesn't work**? Your dog's frustration will rise and his social skills will deteriorate. Dogs *want* to

be around other dogs on some level, even if they are afraid or socially awkward.

- Asking your dog to "Sit" or "Watch me" or other obedience commands while the other dog or person is in view.

  - **Why this doesn't work?** If your dog is too stressed, he cannot calm himself down and then perform a behavior. He is also in a more vulnerable position, which can increase anxiety.

- Blocking your dog with your body while the other dog or person is in view.

  - **Why this doesn't work?** Just blocking a trigger does not make it go away. Your dog's frustration or fear is still present.

- Shocking, choking, yelling at your dog.

  - **Why this doesn't work?** It might *seem* like it works initially since your dog *might* stop barking, but you are punishing signals which can lead to more problems. A dog barks, growls, snaps, or bites for a reason, and these are all warnings to another creature to move away. If you suppress warning signals, your dog may bite without warning. Focus on getting your dog comfortable, not punishing him for acting like a dog.

A REMINDER ABOUT WHAT DOES WORK

- Lead your dog in the "Y" or "T" pattern until your dog becomes less interested in the other dog.

- Find a neutral location where your dog can observe dogs at a safe distance where he immediately turns towards you when you, 'click' and then he takes a treat.

BORING? GOOD!

If you feel bored or if the training is uneventful, that is a good sign! If your dog is periodically barking and then quiets, it means that frustration is building. Do not feel bad if your dog initially barks and you have to move him frequently. That will happen until you make progress and understand the proper distances and movement that your dog needs to remain calm. Boring and uneventful are the long-term goals, not the initial result.

YOUR DOG WILL BE MORE RELAXED

One by-product of uneventful interactions is that your dog will be more relaxed because of more mental stimulation. When dogs react to every dog, it becomes routine:

"I see a dog. I bark at the dog."

Your dog isn't doing a lot of thinking or evaluation. However, when you keep your dog farther away at a distance where he isn't triggered and becomes reactive, he "forces" himself to evaluate the situation more. I have had clients remark that they have never seen their dog as tired as after our successful desensitization training session. Often their dog isn't even moving much or exerting a lot of physical exercise, but mentally they are exhausted.

Dogs that bark a lot, get reactive on a leash, or are always around other barking dogs at daycare may find it hard to calm down.

START FAR AWAY AND MOVE CLOSER

If your dog reacts when you start too close, it becomes more difficult to desensitize because your dog is already stressed. If your dog reacts agitated frequently, it's best to find bigger spaces to walk and train. Unfortunately, the closest location to your home might not be the best place to desensitize your dog. Use your neighborhood for bathroom breaks and get your dog in the car and take him to a location where you have more space. Eventually, you should be able to work in your neighborhood and see results as well.

You should train yourself to MOVE immediately if your dog shows any signs of agitation. The less time (seconds matter) that your dog is in a stressful situation, the better. MOVE.

SKATEBOARD-HATING PUG

It is important to start far away from triggers and avoid an emotional roller coaster resulting in frustration and reactivity. In Chicago, I had a client with a wonderful two-year-old Pug that was friendly on leash until a skateboard appeared. We met at a skate park so I could show my client how to address this problem. We both parked about thirty yards away from the skate park and exited our cars. As soon as Jake, the Pug, heard the skateboards, he turned towards them and went ballistic.

He barked, snarled and pulled on the leash as if he were an eighty pound Rottweiler.

We immediately moved him away from the park until he stopped barking. We had to move another twenty yards away before he stopped. He had no interest in the clicker or treats, even at this distance. We crept closer to evaluate his response. He immediately started barking again and would not calm down.

We stopped the session and rescheduled for a later date. The next session, we both parked much farther away, at a distance where Jake was calm. We could move closer to the park at that point, and he remained under control. My client worked diligently on this problem and Jake eventually could be at a reasonable distance away from skateboards and remain calm. It took a lot of work since his level of anxiety was so high.

The takeaway was that once Jake got so agitated, he could not calm down and there was no way to find a starting point to desensitize him. Once he was over threshold, he was "done."

SUMMARY

- Understand your dog's baseline behavior before encountering other dogs.
- As soon as your dog sees another dog, 'click' and attempt to give a treat.
- If he doesn't turn around and take the treat immediately, move to a new location or move him quickly back and forth at a safe distance to allow him to say, "Hello" and mitigate frustration.
- Wait until he turns away from the other dog, which indicates that you can stop moving or move back for another safe pass.
- Be conservative with your distances when working around triggers. You will make more progress if your dog remains calm from the beginning to the end of the training exercise.
- Lead your dog away if they stop responding to the 'click' rather than pulling them back.
- Stop using the clicker if your dog becomes highly agitated and doesn't respond to it.
- Avoiding all dogs can increase frustration and hinder social skills.

Chapter 13
SUMMARY OF STRATEGIES SO FAR

Read on for a summary followed by more tips and exercises. Hopefully, this helps clarify questions you have. I also have **Troubleshooting** and **FAQ** sections at the back of the book.

POSITIONING AND MOVEMENT

Desensitizing your dog to other dogs requires patience, strategy, and consistent effort. This guide will walk you through a proven approach to help your dog become more comfortable and less reactive when encountering other dogs.

INITIAL STEPS: FIND A SUITABLE LOCATION

- Begin the desensitization process by selecting a location where you can control the distance between your dog and other dogs. This could be a sidewalk, park, or any well-trafficked area with dogs passing by.
- Begin with a distance of at least twenty to thirty feet away from other dogs. This distance provides a buffer for your dog to observe other dogs without feeling overwhelmed.
- Use a clicker or a verbal marker as soon as your dog notices another dog. Immediately follow the 'click' with a treat. This creates a positive association.

Positioning

> ## Position yourself so your dog is between you and the other dog. 'Click' as soon as your dog sees him. Rotate your body as he walks by and 'click' each time your dog looks at him.

PAY ATTENTION TO POSITIONING

- **Move to the Side:** If an approaching dog is too close, lead your dog to the side of the path.
- **Everything is in Front of You:** You should be able to see your dog and then the other dog in a straight line.
- **Move to Stay in the Correct Position:** As dogs walk by, pivot so your dog remains in front of you, closer to the other dog.

OBSERVE YOUR DOG'S RESPONSE

- Pay attention to your dog's behavior. Did your dog turn toward you after hearing the click, or did she ignore the clicker, bark, lunge or other response which indicates she isn't calm.

- Based on your dog's reaction, you have two choices: stay in place if your dog responds positively, or lead your dog away if she is reactive. Avoid pulling your dog forcefully.

LEADING AWAY VS. PULLING BACK

- Lead your dog away by gently guiding her in a safe "Y" or "T" direction. This minimizes tension on the leash and reduces stress for your dog.

- Pulling your dog back creates tension and fear, potentially making your dog appear aggressive. Leading her away reduces stress.

ILLUSTRATED COMPARISON: LEADING VS. PULLING

The next illustration demonstrates leading versus pulling your dog. Leading allows you to guide your dog while reducing a tight leash, reducing stress, frustration and reactivity.

CHOOSING THE RIGHT DIRECTION TO MOVE

- Move your dog laterally, following the top of a "Y" or a "T" to create distance from the other dog. This approach minimizes tension on the leash and helps your dog feel less stressed.

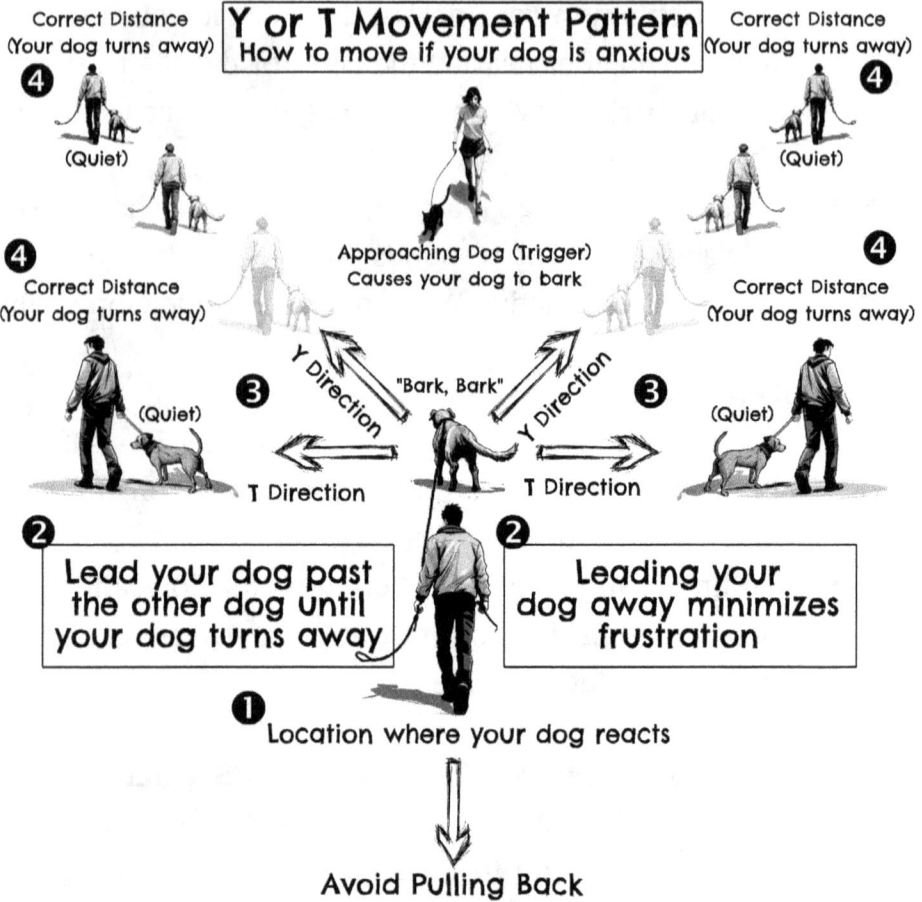

Y or T Movement Pattern
How to move if your dog is anxious

Correct Distance
(Your dog turns away)
❹
(Quiet)

Correct Distance
(Your dog turns away)
❹
(Quiet)

Correct Distance
(Your dog turns away)
❹
(Quiet)

Approaching Dog (Trigger)
Causes your dog to bark

Correct Distance
(Your dog turns away)
❹
(Quiet)

❸
Y Direction
"Bark, Bark"
Y Direction
❸

T Direction
T Direction

❷
Lead your dog past
the other dog until
your dog turns away

❷
Leading your
dog away minimizes
frustration

❶
Location where your dog reacts

Avoid Pulling Back

- Move your dog from the other dog until she looks away
  from the other dog. This indicates a demeanor shift, or
  change in focus.

STAY OR MOVE?

- **Correct Position:** If your dog responds positively to the
  clicker, stay where you are or move closer to the other

dog. If your dog is calm, you should stay where you are if the other dog is moving towards you.

- **Need to Move:** If your dog gets agitated or stops taking treats, lead her away from the other dog until you see a demeanor shift. This prevents heightened stress levels.

- If your dog doesn't turn around, but takes treats, be more cautious and ready to move if she gets more stressed.

MOVE UNTIL YOU SEE A DEMEANOR SHIFT

- **Movement is Natural.** Movement is one choice that dogs make when they are feeling threatened. Leading your dog away will reduce stress due to increased distance and physical exercise.

- **Look for a Demeanor Shift.** Once your dog turns away, you can stop, wait until your dog looks at the other dog, and 'click,' or lead your dog past for another safe greeting.

SOMETIMES LOTS OF LAPS ARE NECESSARY

- **Movement is Never a Bad Idea.** If your dog is anxious and you have enough space, making multiple passes back and forth is an effective strategy. Continue moving your dog during each pass until she shows a demeanor shift and turns away from the other dog.

- **Shift Should Happen Closer.** As you continue moving back and forth, often you will notice your dog's demeanor shift happening sooner or closer to the other dog.

UNDERSTAND THRESHOLD AND ADJUSTMENTS

- Identify the distance at which your dog reacts to other dogs. This distance is their *threshold*.
- Work below your dog's threshold and edge closer to the other dog as she becomes more comfortable. Adjust the distance based on her reactions.

STRIVING FOR CALM WALKS

- The goal is to make each walk less stressful for your dog. Adjust the distance and your strategy based on her progress.
- Analyze each interaction and make adjustments as needed.

By following these steps, you will help your dog become desensitized to other dogs and achieve calmer and more enjoyable walks. Remember, every positive interaction is a step toward a happier and less reactive dog.

Chapter 14
FINE-TUNE YOUR TRAINING

If your dog is friendly, but socially awkward and gets too excited when she sees another dog, that can lead to problems. The excitement can lead to frustration and cause over-exuberant responses. Pulling, whining and barking are annoying by themselves, but you don't want another dog attacking your dog if she is wild and looks like a potential threat. If she gets attacked, she might become fearful of dogs instead of just socially awkward.

LOWER FRUSTRATION
Frustration leads to amplified behaviors. Always move your dog if she is frustrated. If you are walking behind another dog, avoid "battling" your dog and thinking about this as an obedience problem if she wants to be near the other dog. Work on leash pulling after you reduce her frustration. If you have enough space to safely move past the other dog, do this and then find a location off to the side where you can 'click' and treat when your dog looks back at the other dog as the other dog walks by.

Pass to Reduce Frustration

Starting Point
Frustrated Dog

"Hello"

"Hello"

Ending Point
Less Frustrated Dog

Dog turned
away after she
was allowed to
say "Hello"

If you are behind another dog
and your dog is pulling, move
forward at a safe distance to
reduce frustration.

WHEN YOUR FRIENDLY DOG SEES ANOTHER DOG

The calmer your dog is during interactions with other dogs, the better the outcome. When you see another dog, you have two options:

1. Your dog will interact and greet the other dog.
2. You will keep your dog away from the other dog and walk past.

Whether or not your dog interacts with the other dog, Step One, desensitizing your dog as you approach, applies to every situation. After that, you need to decide whether the two dogs will interact. If the other dog is reactive, old, sick, or unfamiliar to you, it's best to keep moving. Avoid putting your dog in a situation where it will go badly and your dog has a traumatic experience.

FOUR-STEP GREETINGS

Here are the four steps to follow if your dog is friendly. You should practice this even if your dog frequently interacts with the other dog that she is approaching. The goal here is to lower reactivity and frustration, so greetings go more smoothly. If your dog is aggressive, you can still follow this model, you just won't allow any greeting or contact. Instead, you will simply lead your dog away.

You should pull your dog to the side and 'click' and treat from a stationary position. Don't ask your dog to "sit" or any other behavior. Stand behind your dog with your dog closer to the oncoming dog so you can see if he responds to the 'click,' or is more interested in the other dog.

1. **DESENSITIZE.** 'Click' and treat AS SOON as your dog sees the other dog. Continue 'clicking' and treating every time your dog looks at the other dog until your dog stops paying attention to the clicker and stops taking treats. If he still takes treats but doesn't turn around, you can continue 'clicking' and treating.

2. **INTERACT.** Once your dog stops responding to the clicker, decide whether your dog will interact. Either allow him to interact or keep moving. Brief interactions while moving past reduce the risk of your dog being too wild for the other dog, or the other dog attacking your dog. See the **Click, Move, Treat** section for more guidance.

3. **OBEDIENCE.** While your dog is interacting with the other dog, occasionally ask for a "Let's Go" command. Say, "Let's Go" one time and gently guide your dog away

from the other dog. Either 'click' and treat him or just say, "Good!" and then, "Go Play!" and lead him back to the other dog. The goal is that even if he is playing with another dog, he will still listen to your commands.

4.   **DESENSITIZE.** When the play session is over, 'click' and treat each time your dog looks at the other dog walking away. Dogs can get frustrated when their friend walks away. This strategy desensitizes him to the frustration of his friend leaving. In my experience, frustrated dogs can become more reactive when encountering the next dog.

SHOULD THEY GREET?

I am very hesitant to allow my dogs to meet dogs that I don't know. Many trainers suggest never letting your dog interact with other dogs on walks. You need to decide what is safe for your dog.

Some signs that you should keep walking and not let your dog interact:

•   The person hesitates after you ask if their dog is friendly. It is difficult for some people to admit their dog is reactive. They might also want to "try one more time" to see how their dog reacts. Don't let your dog be a guinea pig with an unknown dog.

- The person sees you and immediately chokes up on the leash.
- The other dog is intensely staring at your dog.
- The other dog is licking her lips.
- The other dog's tail drops.

CLICK, MOVE, TREAT

How do you progress from your dog being ten feet from another dog to touch nose-to-nose or possibly even playing with another dog? You can safely use the **Click, Move, Treat** strategy.

Practice this strategy at any distance, but it's most useful when there is a history of calm interactions at a safe distance and you want to assess if your dogs can get closer. You should adjust your expectations based on what is currently happening with your dog. If your dog is barking or growling at ten feet away, you should probably be twenty to thirty feet or more away from another dog. You can't force your dog to be calm. Use this for your fine-tuning once your dog has a lot of exposure to dogs and is consistent and calm. Practice this strategy only if you've practiced reading your dog's body language and there haven't been any incidents of lunging, air snapping, or biting another dog.

The Click, Move, Treat strategy is a more advanced version of the strategy previously discussed **Multiple Passes Strategy** shown below. If you are near a brand new dog, or if your dog has higher reactivity, you should be more cautious with your distances and use the Multiple Passes Strategy.

Multiple Passes To Lower Reactivity

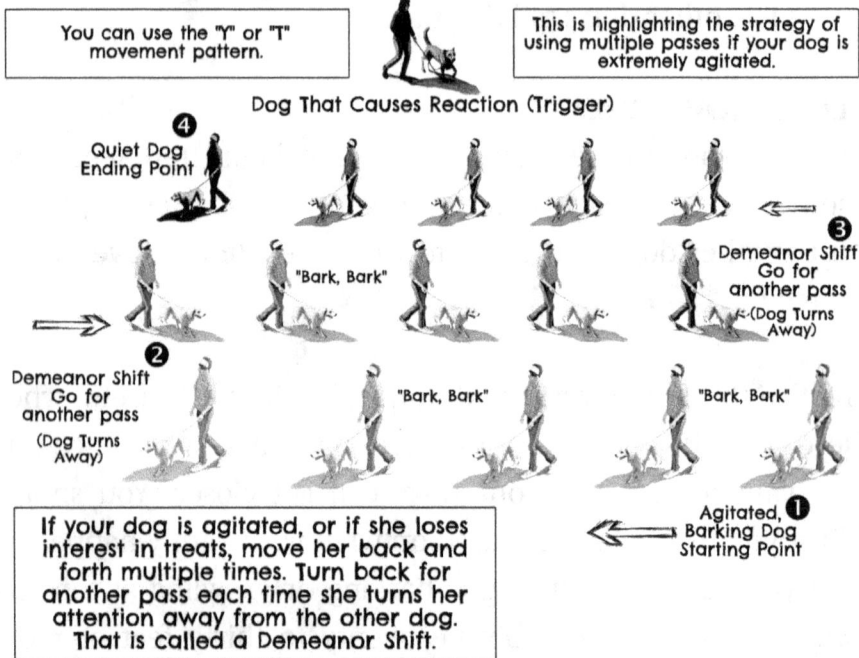

You can use the "Y" or "T" movement pattern.

This is highlighting the strategy of using multiple passes if your dog is extremely agitated.

Dog That Causes Reaction (Trigger)

4 Quiet Dog Ending Point

"Bark, Bark"

3 Demeanor Shift Go for another pass

(Dog Turns Away)

2 Demeanor Shift Go for another pass

(Dog Turns Away)

"Bark, Bark"

"Bark, Bark"

If your dog is agitated, or if she loses interest in treats, move her back and forth multiple times. Turn back for another pass each time she turns her attention away from the other dog. That is called a Demeanor Shift.

1 Agitated, Barking Dog Starting Point

Once your dog is calmer, you can try the Click, Move, Treat Strategy. I also call this my Serpentine Approach, since it looks like a snake. This method answers the question of, "Now that my dog seems more comfortable with another dog, what can I do to evaluate whether they can safely interact with each other?"

The strategy is to keep your dog moving and avoid situations that make him or the other dog nervous. You should not pause or stop walking until you have more evidence of calm interactions. This is easiest if the other dog is stationary, either sitting or standing. The steps are:

1. Walk by the other dog without pausing, making sure that the two dogs are at least five feet away from each other – you should be on the "outside" of the action with your dog closer to the other dog.
2. 'Click' when your dog looks at the other dog.
3. After the 'click,' gently immediately move your dog to a safe distance (typically three to four steps away).
4. Give your dog a tasty treat.
5. Evaluate both dog's responses.
6. Repeat.

You should ensure you are practicing safe leash handling as described previously. Make sure one hand is through the loop of your leash and the other hand is completely empty (no clicker or treat). You should use your empty hand as your "steering" and "brake." Always hold the leash loosely and gently guide or stop your dog if he lunges. This is your safest option to avoid surprises.

The **Click, Move, Treat Strategy** is shown on the following page.

Serpentine Approach Strategy
'CLICK', MOVE, TREAT

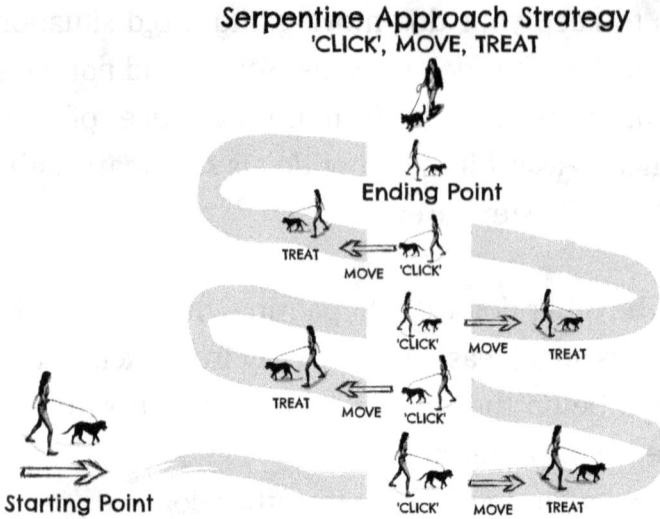

Ending Point

TREAT ⇐ MOVE 'CLICK'

'CLICK' MOVE ⇒ TREAT

TREAT ⇐ MOVE 'CLICK'

Starting Point ⇒

'CLICK' MOVE ⇒ TREAT

Use this strategy to safely move closer to other dogs. This prevents head-on greetings, focuses on constant movement, and avoids putting a treat between two dogs which sometimes results in a fight.	'Click' when your dog looks at the other dog. Keep moving and offer a treat a few steps past that point. Evaluate both dogs to ensure that they are both calm. If so, move one step closer and continue working.

WHY IS IT IMPORTANT TO MOVE AFTER THE 'CLICK'?

This entire process mitigates the risk of having the two dogs too close, too quickly. If your dog responds immediately to the 'click' and takes the treat gently, you can move closer during the next pass. Always make sure that you are on the outside and the two dogs are closer. This allows you to quickly take one step away in case either dog lunges, and also prevents you from tripping over your lunging dog.

Eventually, you should be able to walk by more slowly and allow the dogs to sniff each other. This is where movement is key. You don't want to 'click,' stop moving and put a treat between two dogs. The two dogs might not handle the three to five seconds this takes, and you also don't want to risk the two dogs fighting over the treat. **CLICK** at the closest point, **MOVE** away and **TREAT**.

If your dog can handle the quick sniff, then next time you can walk more slowly and allow them to sniff for a couple seconds. After a couple seconds, **CLICK, MOVE** and **TREAT** and evaluate your dog's response. If both dogs can handle sniffing for a couple of seconds, you can allow them to interact for longer periods of time.

If there is a problem and one or both dogs growls, barks, or snaps, you should be more cautious and add more distance. You can also choose a distance that both dogs are comfortable and go for a pleasant walk, 'clicking' and treating periodically when your dog looks at the other dog.

TALK YOUR DOG THROUGH A SITUATION

As you learn your dog's comfort level with various triggers, you can slowly start moving away from the clicker in some situations. Let's say your dog routinely turns away from other dogs when he hears the 'click' at a distance of fifteen feet.

When you have achieved some reliability at a distance, try "talking your dog through" the situation. Instead of 'clicking' and treating immediately when he looks at another dog, start talking in an encouraging tone of voice. The message that I want you to convey is of excitement. One way to think about what you are communicating is by saying:

"Isn't this fun? There is a dog approaching! It is great when a dog approaches! Remember? That usually means treats and other fun things for you!"

"You are doing great! You don't care about that
other dog at all, do you? I don't even need to 'click'!"

While I usually say, "Good, good, you are doing great, nice job!" etc. I don't want you to think that this is an obedience exercise. You are not saying,

"I know you want to bark at that dog, but thank you for not barking!"

You're trying to make the experience fun and see if your verbal encouragement is enough to prevent your dog from barking. You are still working at the emotional level. Even if you offer your dog steak or encourage them verbally, they will ignore you if they are more interested in another dog. If he isn't concerned about the other dog, he will ignore her and turn towards you to see what all the excitement is about.

If your dog looks at you while you talk excitedly, it means he's not stressed by the other dog's appearance. It means your dog *doesn't care* that the other dog is there. That is the goal! Once you are successful at this, try it periodically when your dog seems calm around another dog.

If this strategy fails miserably, and your dog ends up barking, no problem! Just simply learn from it and:

1) Lead your dog quickly away.

and

2) Find a new location where your dog is calm and continue the process of 'clicking' and treating when your dog looks at the other dog.

Eventually, you will simply use encouragement with your dog around a variety of triggers and use the clicker less. If the situation changes, start 'clicking' and treating again to see if your dog is calm around the new trigger. Examples of new triggers include a dog barking, a dog running by, a new dog appearing, etc.

THE LIFECYCLE OF INTRODUCTIONS

The normal pattern of introducing your dog to triggers is:

1. 'Click' and treat every time he experiences a new trigger to desensitize him, evaluate his reactivity, then adjust his location, if needed.

2. Try using verbal encouragement instead of 'clicks' to see if that alone is enough to distract him and keep him calm as he gets used to a certain intensity.

3. Click and treat when the trigger changes, like when the other dog gets closer, barks, or starts running.

4. Eventually your dog will remain calm without 'clicking' or verbal encouragement and you are "done" desensitizing him to that trigger.

REINFORCER SAMPLING

Once you feel more confident about your dog's comfort around triggers, you can experiment with a technique known as Reinforcer Sampling. This technique can help "lock in" the association between dogs and treats. You can sometimes show the treat upfront but not give it to your dog right away.

Let's say your dog is consistently calm when another dog is thirty feet away. You are not sure, however, about how your dog will react when the other dog is twenty feet away. You can then wave a tasty treat in front of your dog's nose when he is looking at the dog at thirty feet away, but do not give it to him yet. Then, when the other dog gets twenty feet away, 'click' and offer the treat. This reinforces the message that the appearance of dogs = tasty treats and helps create a positive association.

During this process, evaluate your dog's changing reactions. As the other dog approaches, your dog might glance at the other dog, but remain calm. If he gets more agitated as the other dog approaches, then he is not ready for this strategy and you should instead 'click' and treat when he looks at the approaching dog, or move him away.

SUMMARY

- The four-step greeting process provides a framework for friendly interactions with other dogs.
- Use the Click, Move, Treat method to help dogs get closer and potentially play with each other.
- Always watch your dog's reaction to ensure the process isn't stressful, and use safe leash handling by making sure two hands are on the leash.
- Gradually reduce reliance on the clicker as your dog becomes more comfortable with triggers and see if your dog remains calm with verbal encouragement.
- Reinforcer Sampling: Periodically show a treat upfront without giving it right away, and clicking and offering the treat when the other dog gets closer.

Chapter 15
HONE YOUR OBSERVATION SKILLS

🐾

You should now understand how to recognize your dog's stress signals, and determine when you can keep your dog where she is, and when you should move her to a new location. You should also be more knowledgeable in recognizing your dog's stress signals even before using the clicker. Consider the clicker as a tool to help you determine if your dog can handle what is in front of her. If you 'click' and your dog does not turn away from a trigger, that means that trigger might seem threatening to her.

Now let's talk about some other changes that you can look for that can show elevated stress levels. As you go through your day with your dog, I want you to pay close attention to her resting state. What does she look like when she is just relaxing with the family watching TV or playing fetch in the backyard? If she has a tail, what does her relaxed, happy tail look like? Is it up, is it down, does it rest at fifty percent or horizontal to her body, or does it drop when she is relaxed?

What do her ears look like? Are they floppy and relaxed, or stiff and at attention? Are they back or forward? Do they rotate like a radar dish toward noises? Do they move before she barks?

I also want you to notice what happens when the doorbell rings. Does she bark first and then race to the door? Does she look at you first and then stay where she is?

Start watching her on your walks. If a jogger runs by, does your dog look at him? What if there is a child, a stroller, a skateboard? What if she is sniffing the grass, and a trigger appears? Does she calmly continue sniffing? Does she raise her head to look? How long does she stare at the trigger? Does she glance and then go back to sniffing?

Study the **Stress Levels Assessment** and **Body Language** chapters of this book if you need more suggestions on what to look for when evaluating signs of stress.

There have been many times in my dog training career that I have noticed a dog's body language change, explained what I saw to my client and they did not notice it even though we were both closely looking at their dog. I have worked on my observation skills for over two decades, and I still discover new things that dogs do that I never saw before. I have to adapt to each training session quickly and learn a dog's signals as soon as possible. Not only do I want to help my client, I also want to avoid doing something that results in a bite! The good news is that you have only one or a few dogs in your household that you need to study.

The best thing you can do is practice every day by observing your dog and noticing *changes*. Body language changes do not always indicate stress, but it is crucial to ask the right questions. How does your dog's body change when he is calm vs. stressed?

OBSERVATION SKILLS - EXERCISE ONE

This is an exercise that can take you to the next level with your observation skills. The previous chapters recommended you keep your dog calm and stay at a distance where he turns around without hesitation when he hears the 'click.'

This exercise is different. You should do this periodically just to learn more about your dog's body language. This is not something that is your day-to-day strategy. Maybe just use this once a week or every couple of weeks. You should practice this exercise after you have determined your dog's consistent distance needed to be calm around dogs. Let's assume your dog can be comfortable at approximately twenty feet away from another dog. You can use the length of cars, number of houses, or other landmarks to gauge distance as well.

Safety is always the priority. Do not move close enough to the other dog so your dog can sniff, and possibly bite, another dog. I designed this so you can fine-tune your observation skills at a safe distance. If your dog is comfortable at twenty feet away, try positioning your dog a few feet closer near a path where dogs walk by. Make sure that you are not close enough where the other person allows their dogs to say, "Hello," and risk a bad interaction. It's best to have someone with you when watching your dog, to notice body language and communicate with other owners not to get too close.

If your dog is really anxious, move him away. He should not experience a lot of stress. You are attempting to create a *slightly* stressful situation for him to observe his subtle signals and learn more. After you position your dog at the closer distance, simply watch your dog as dogs pass by. Unlike the other exercises where he is in front of you, you want to learn as much information as possible so you should position yourself so you can see his face. Off to the side a bit is good, but do not block him, so he can't see triggers as they appear. If you have a helper, have them hold the leash so you can watch from the front.

You can also use a video camera and analyze it later. If you are by yourself, you can set up a tripod and capture all kinds of glorious details! The slow motion option on a lot of cameras is very useful. Watch and learn. As the other dog gets closer, your dog will *do something*. I want you to gather as much detail as possible about the *changes* in your dog's behavior. As each dog walks by, look at different parts of your dog to learn how the appearance of the other dog causes physiological changes in your dog.

You can observe his eyes, mouth, tail, breathing rate, and body position to determine if he is alert or relaxed. Does his head stay still, or does it move up, down, or side to side? Look at his ears. Do they move, or do they remain still? Does he maintain eye contact for an unusually long time? If you can see his pupils, do they dilate? This indicates stress.

After a couple of dogs have passed, move to a distance where you think he will be totally comfortable. If the previous comfort zone started at twenty feet from other dogs, move thirty feet or more to ensure that he is totally comfortable. Since he was just in a bit of a stressful situation, you probably need to add some distance to keep him calm since he might be a bit on edge.

Now at the farther distance, watch him again. You should see calm, neutral body language at this distance. Compare what you saw at the closer distance to learn what subtle signs of stress show up when your dog is too close to other dogs.

Then, move forward a few feet and try it again. See any more changes? You are learning!

OBSERVATION SKILLS - EXERCISE TWO

Now you will do a similar exercise, but you will 'click' when you see the signs of stress.

The goal for this exercise is you should increase your understanding about the stress signals your dog is presenting. For instance, if you saw your dog lower his tail in the last exercise and you think that is a stressful response, you might prove this.

Look for body language signals like head movement downward, stiffening body, wide eyes, increased breathing, still tail, etc.

- Position your dog at the same distance as Exercise One. If your dog is normally non-reactive towards dogs at twenty feet from the walking path, perhaps you are eighteen feet away, or just barely over his comfort zone.

- It is fine for this if you are a bit to the side of your dog instead of behind him so you can see more of his facial expressions.
- Ideally, you have someone else to help you also watch your dog from the front to see his facial expressions.
- AS SOON as you see one of the previously identified signals you think denotes stress, 'click' and note what your dog does.

As you previously learned, the reaction after hearing the 'click' and the movement and interest in the treat can signify if he is comfortable or stressed.

- If he jerks quickly towards the clicker, he is more stressed than if he moves more slowly or casually
- If he takes the treat roughly, he is stressed
- If he doesn't turn around immediately, he is stressed
- If he doesn't turn around at all, he is stressed

An additional known stressful response (such as taking the treat roughly) after a possible stress signal (hard stare) confirms the initial change in behavior was a sign of stress!

HOW CAN YOU USE THIS INFORMATION?
The next time you see the hard stare, for instance, you can move your dog away even before you 'click.' You just learned

the hard stare means that your dog is stressed, so you don't need to 'click' the next time you witness this. Just move him away! Moving your dog to a new location as soon as you observe any signs of stress even before 'clicking' is the final goal in successfully understanding how to lower your dog's anxiety. Why is this important?

To lower anxiety, you want your dog to be in stressful situations for less time. Seconds add up over the course of the walk. You can reduce your dog's stress levels by removing them before their stress levels increase (before you 'click' vs. after), which will result in less stress for your dog.

Think how that can add up. If your dog sees twelve dogs during your walks in one day and you remove him each time five seconds sooner, that is one minute less stress. Over the course of a week, that is seven minutes. And that is just dogs! What if your dog is reactive to kids, skateboards, the mail carrier, trucks, and motorcycles? Your dog might be exposed to twenty or thirty triggers each walk. If you improve your observation skills and keep your dog within his comfort zone, he will experience less arousal and anxiety.

This brings up the point of exposure. Some of my clients hardly see any dogs on their walks. If that is the case with you, bring your dog to parks, near walking paths, or outside of dog parks where there are more dogs. The ideal location will have plenty of space to move your dog farther away if he gets stressed.

Some paths in North Carolina where I live are too "tight" and are counter-productive because dogs get anxious each time they are on that path. I suggest to my clients that they work elsewhere until their dog is more comfortable and then try that path later.

SUMMARY

- Observe your dog's behavior: Watch your dog's reactions and body language focusing on various indicators like eyes, mouth, tail, and breathing.
- Gradual exposure and comparison: After observing at a closer distance, gradually move to a farther distance and note the changes in your dog's behavior.
- Conduct a similar exercise to Exercise One, but instead of just looking for signs of stress, 'click' when you observe signs of stress.
- If your dog hesitates, doesn't take the treat, takes the treat roughly or barks then you have successfully identified a subtle sign of stress.
- Next time you see this behavior, move him away before you 'click' to prevent an escalation of stress levels.

Chapter 16
STRUCTURED WALKING EXERCISES

Use the strategies you've learned to interact with other dogs you see on walks. You should also enlist the help of a friend to practice structured greeting exercises. A "greeting" could be at a distance of twenty feet or more from another dog, based on how calm your dog is. Here are some suggestions for working with another dog.

It is important to strive to work below both dogs' threshold. If one or both dogs become scared, you will make less progress than if both dogs remain calm. Take your time. It might take many sessions before the dogs can sniff, if ever.

Don't worry if your dog initially starts barking as long as you have space to move him away and you eventually see progress where he calms down. If he is barking continuously and getting more agitated, you are doing more harm than good and you need to move farther away.

MOVEMENT, MOVEMENT, MOVEMENT
There is no exception to this rule for every strategy in this book. If your dog cannot handle the current situation because of fear or frustration, the ONLY option is to move to a location

where he can be calm. Nothing magical is happening during movement except you are simply finding a location where your dog doesn't care as much about the other dog. At that point, the clicker "works." He will start paying attention to it and taking treats, and he is getting desensitized to the other dog.

These exercises will help you learn more about how your dog reacts to other dogs based on different factors. You can practice any of these exercises depending on your location and proximity of other dogs.

With each exercise, position the two dogs closer to one another with each person on the outside. You should 'click' and attempt to give your dog a treat when he looks at the other dog. If he easily turns away from the other dog and takes the treat gently, take one step closer to the other dog.

Always use movement to prevent the two dogs from being too close for too much time. Make sure both hands are on the leash to guide your dog away if needed.

These suggestions are relevant whether you are practicing a structured greeting with a friend and their dog, or you see a random dog on a walk or in the park.

Your dog should be
closer to the other dog so
you can see everything
in front of you.

MULTIPLE PASSES BACK AND FORTH

When introducing your dog to another dog, you may need to move them back and forth at different distances until they feel calm. Don't get frustrated with this process. The key is that you are moving AS SOON as your dog gets agitated, while still allowing your dog to interact safely with the other dog. Eventually, your dog should calm down.

If your dog responds to the 'click' by turning around and taking a treat, you can continue working in that location. If not, move farther away. Once you move to a location where your dog responds to the 'click,' then you can stay there and move closer to the other dog step by step.

Multiple passes step-by-step process:

1. When you see another dog approaching, watch your dog.
2. 'Click' when your dog looks at the other dog.
3. If your dog doesn't take the treat, roughly takes the treat, or starts barking, stop using the clicker and move past the other dog, using the "Y" or "T" movement pattern, if you have enough room to do this safely.
4. Make sure your dog is between you and the other dog, so he does not trip you.
5. Keep both hands on the leash so you can safely guide him past.
6. When your dog turns away from the other dog, stop moving.
7. Reposition yourself so you are standing behind your dog.
8. Use the clicker again and 'click' when your dog looks at the other dog.
9. If your dog responds to the 'click' and takes the treat gently, that is the correct location for desensitization.
10. You can stay there or move closer to the other dog.
11. If your dog does not respond to the 'click,' does not take the treat, takes the treat roughly or barks, repeat step #3 above.

See the illustration on the following page.

Multiple Passes To Lower Reactivity

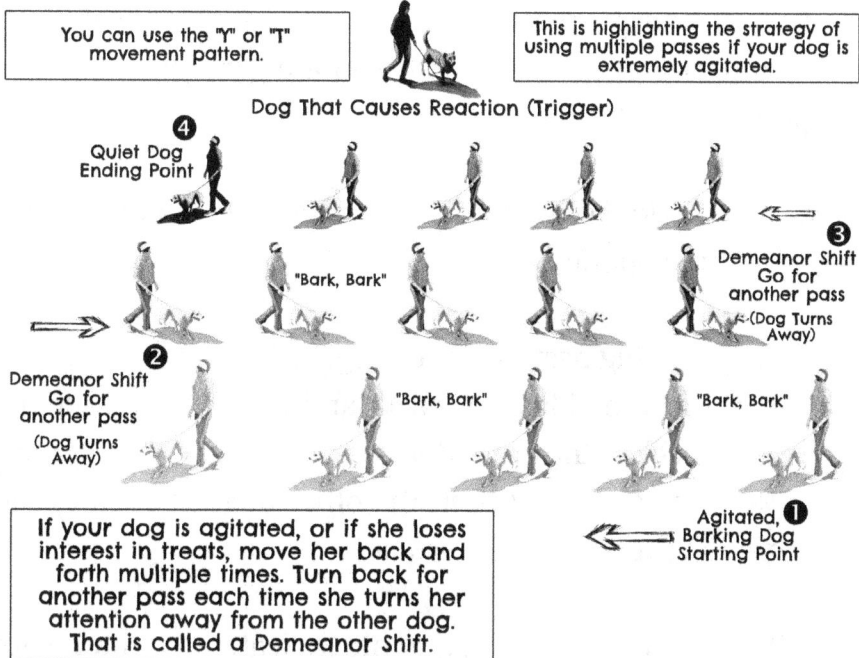

You can use the "Y" or "T" movement pattern.

This is highlighting the strategy of using multiple passes if your dog is extremely agitated.

Dog That Causes Reaction (Trigger)

4 Quiet Dog Ending Point

3 Demeanor Shift Go for another pass (Dog Turns Away)

"Bark, Bark"

2 Demeanor Shift Go for another pass (Dog Turns Away)

"Bark, Bark"

"Bark, Bark"

1 Agitated, Barking Dog Starting Point

If your dog is agitated, or if she loses interest in treats, move her back and forth multiple times. Turn back for another pass each time she turns her attention away from the other dog. That is called a Demeanor Shift.

PASS IF YOUR DOG IS FRUSTRATED

If you are walking behind another dog and it frustrates your dog wanting to get closer, pass the other dog instead of pulling your dog back. Do not worry about loose leash walking at this moment when your dog is highly distracted. As long as you can safely control your dog, it doesn't matter if your dog is pulling during this interaction. Your goal is simply to allow your dog to say, "Hello" at a safe distance, mitigate frustration and move past the other dog until your dog calms down.

Whether your dog is frustrated and friendly or nervous and aggressive, this is useful. Dogs want to be closer to another dog either way. Make sure you have enough room to safely move past the other dog. Your dog should be between you and the other dog so he doesn't trip you if he lunges. Make sure both your hands are on the leash and you are gently guiding your dog past.

Once your dog looks away from the other dog (demeanor shift) you have three options:

- Keep moving past the other dog.
- Move to the side and 'click' and treat when your dog looks back at the other dog.
- Move towards, and past, the other dog for another safe greeting at the proper distance.

The "Hello" in the following graphic indicates any interaction the two dogs might have. The two dogs could be:

- interested and quiet
- interested and barking
- nervous, aggressive and barking

The key point to remember is that frustrated dogs *want* to interact with another dog. Pulling them back increases frustration. Moving your dog past another dog allows the dogs to interact and your job is to keep moving until your dog turns away from the other dog. This indicates your dog is less interested. Multiple passes back and forth will eventually calm a dog down, assuming there is enough space where they can safely pass each other without a risk of a bite.

There needs to be enough space to accomplish this safely whenever you pass another dog. If your dog reacts often in a crowded place, find a different location to walk them until they are calm enough to be closer to other dogs.

Even if your dog barks at the other dog, he should eventually calm down and be quiet. Finding the proper distance is a key element to this strategy.

Pass to Reduce Frustration

Starting Point
Frustrated Dog

"Hello"

"Hello"

Ending Point
Less Frustrated Dog

Dog turned
away after she
was allowed to
say "Hello"

If you are behind another dog and your dog is pulling, move forward at a safe distance to reduce frustration.

FOLLOW

Following another dog is less intimidating. One strategy I frequently use is to cross the street as a dog is approaching, and then cross back and follow once they pass by. Use this strategy if the other dog is getting too close. If you have the space to cross the street safely, that is a better strategy than staying where you are if it results in your dog getting stressed.

'Click' and treat when your dog looks at the other dog, and slow down and create more distance if your dog ignores the 'click.'

You can also try passing the other dog if your dog gets frustrated and moving to the side to continue desensitizing your dog after he says, "Hello."

Follow

It is much less intimidating for a dog to follow another dog. 'Click' and treat when your dog looks at the other dog.

HEAD-ON PASS

When passing dog's head on, assess your dog's stress levels and continue moving if he is not calm. Leave enough space to pass safely and have one hand looped through the handle of the leash with your other hand holding the leash approximately halfway towards your dog. Pass the other dog until your dog turns away. Then, you can stop walking, reposition yourself and 'click' when your dog looks back at the other dog.

Head-On Pass

Approaching head-on can be intimidating. Stay at a safe distance and keep moving. 'Click' when your dog looks at the other dog. If your dog ignores the 'click' or barks, keep moving until he turns away from the other dog.

SPEED OF APPROACH

Speed of triggers is one important variable to always consider when evaluating your dog's reactions. If you are working with a friend and their dog, have them increase the speed of their movement if your dog is comfortable with a normal walking speed. Dogs can easily get triggered by faster movements. 'Click' and treat each time your dog looks at the other dog. If your dog cannot handle the faster speed, work at a slower speed and build up to the final velocity.

Speed of Approach

Experiment with the other dog moving at various speeds. This can make a big difference in your dog's stress levels.

ANGLE OF APPROACH

Dogs can react differently depending on the angle of approach of the other dog. Have your friend approach you and your dog from different angles and as soon as your dog looks at the other dog, 'click' and treat. Notice if there is any difference in your dog's reactions based on different angles of approach. As shown in the Proper Positioning example below, you should always be on the "outside" of the action with your dog closer to the other dog.

Angle of Approach

Experiment with different angles of approach. 'Click' and treat every time your dog looks at the other dog.

REMEMBER PROPER POSITIONING

When dogs are passing by during these exercises, remember to rotate your body and keep your dog in front of you. If your dog turns away from the other dog when he hears the 'click', it means that you are at the proper distance so your dog is not too interested or nervous. If your dog is stressed, you should move to a different location and try again.

Positioning

Position yourself so your dog is between you and the other dog. 'Click' as soon as your dog sees him. Rotate your body as he walks by and 'click' each time your dog looks at him.

PARALLEL WALK

At any point during the exercises, you can try a parallel walk and 'click' and treat when your dog looks at the other dog. If both dogs are working on remaining calm, both handlers should use this strategy. You can always move faster ahead or add more space between the two dogs.

During the walk, one person can walk ahead, stop and allow the other person to move past. Each person can periodically try this with their dog. This allows for the two dogs to see each other at different angles, speeds and distances. Each person can 'click' and treat when their dog looks at the other dog.

Parallel Walk

> ## Once you have evaluated both dog's comfort, you can choose a distance and walk the dogs side-by-side

SUMMARY

Utilize dog interactions during walks or involve a friend for structured greetings, maintaining distance based on your dog's behavior.

- **Movement is Essential:** Movement is crucial for all strategies. If your dog can't handle a situation due to fear or frustration, move to a location where your dog is less concerned about the other dog.
- **Pass to Minimize Frustration:** If your dog is frustrated and wants to approach another dog, try passing the other dog at a safe distance instead of pulling away. The goal is to keep moving until your dog turns away from the other dog.
- **Follow:** Following another dog is less intimidating, and you can use it when dogs pass you.

- **Head on Pass:** Can be challenging for dogs, so check your dog's stress levels, keep a safe distance, and keep moving until they are calm.
- **Speed and Angle of Approach:** Consider the speed and angle of the approach of the other dog. Dogs can react differently based on these factors, so adjust the approach accordingly.
- **Proper Positioning is Key:** Maintain proper positioning with your dog in front of you during exercises.
- **Go For a Walk:** A parallel walk is also an option to help dogs remain calm and see each other from different angles, speeds, and distances.

Chapter 17
LEASH SKILLS

🐾

All the movement and positioning strategies can be practiced using a long leash when you have enough space to stay at a safe distance from dogs. Long leashes come in lengths of ten to one hundred feet. I typically use fifteen or thirty foot leashes.

There are many benefits for using a long leash:

- **Less Frequent Tight Leash.** A tight leash creates more anxiety and a long leash allows more movement, reducing the frequency of a tight leash.
- **Evaluate Your Dog's Movement.** If your dog stays close to you while using a long leash, it means he's not interested in the other dog and you're at a safe distance.
- **Obedience Opportunities.** If your dog is calm, you can use this opportunity to work on Recall (Come), Let's Go, or other obedience commands.

There have been many situations where I have worked with a stressed dog and he calms down considerably when I use a long leash. Since the leash is tight less frequently it reduces stress.

If you can safely manipulate your dog, practice the strategies that you have learned to use the "Y" or "T" movements. It can take a bit of time to feel confident using this type of leash, but the benefits make it worth it. Always make sure you are ready with your free hand to guide or stop your dog.

PREY DRIVE
Some dogs have an intense prey drive that creates unique challenges. Desensitization works well if you can control the situation, but it's difficult when animals move quickly.

Here is my suggested approach when working with dogs that have a high prey drive. This is not a quick fix and can take time to see results. Repetition is crucial for a successful desensitization strategy, but it's impossible to schedule training sessions with the different critters in your neighborhood. At times, they may get too close to your dog, which can make your dog anxious and cause their behavior to worsen.

Try this:

1. When you see a squirrel or other critter, stop walking and watch your dog's head.
2. As soon as she sees the squirrel, 'click' and attempt to give a treat. As long as she turns around and takes the treat after the 'click', continue this strategy.
3. If she is too distracted, and doesn't turn around when you 'click,' stop using the clicker. Instead of desensitization, you will now work on obedience.
4. Use two hands and bring the leash up to your chest gently.
5. Walk slowly towards the squirrel while watching your dog.
6. As soon as she takes one step towards the squirrel, say, "Stop" and gently stop her. Do not jerk her back. There is no need to be rough.
7. As soon as she is stationary (because you gently stopped her), say, "Good!" and repeat this process taking one step forward at a time as long as the squirrel is within sight, asking for a "Stop" and gently stopping her each time she moves forward.

WHAT DOES THIS ACCOMPLISH?
If you practice enough, your dog can lose interest in the various critters since she never completes her desire to chase

or eat them. This takes a lot of repetition to achieve this. You should also practice "Stop" in other less distracting situations to give her more practice and create a conditioned response.

SUGGESTIONS FOR PRACTICING "STOP"
Any moment where she is "locked in" to a target and is interested in something is an excellent opportunity to practice, "Stop." She should always be on a leash so you can use it if she doesn't respond to the command.

If she is not too distracted, add the 'click' and treat when you stop her. If she is too distracted and doesn't pay attention to the clicker or take the treat in that situation, just say, "Good" and allow her to move closer to the distraction slowly after each "Good." I like to wait for a superb response, before allowing final access to the location, object or person. If she is too distracted, move farther away to achieve that response. Eventually her performance will improve and she should stop close to the distraction.

When she is not too distracted and responds to the 'click,' the exercise looks like this.
- Put her on leash.
- Wait for her to move towards a tree, toy, treat, person or other distraction.
- Say, "Stop" ONE TIME.
- Gently stop her using the leash.
- 'Click' or say, "Yes" AS SOON as she is stationary – even though she stopped because of the tight leash.

- Give her a treat

If she doesn't turn around initially but still takes the treat it means she is too close to the distraction. Move her farther away and try again. Eventually she will hear the command, "Stop" and turn around before hitting the end of the leash or hearing the 'click.'

Examples of distractions include:
- When she is approaching a tree to sniff
- When she is walking up to her food bowl
- When she wants to greet her favorite person at the front door
- When she is walking towards her favorite playmate outside
- Put a toy on the ground and walk her up to it, stopping her along the way
- Put a treat, chew or food puzzle on the ground and walk her up to it, stopping her along the way

LEASH WALKING STRATEGIES
This book primarily focuses on lowering reactions to triggers. If you need more obedience suggestions not covered in this book, you should find a reputable positive reinforcement dog trainer in your area and take a private lesson or a class.

Making sure your dog receives a proper dose of mental exercise each day is an important part of having a happy, calm dog.

I wanted to share some leash walking strategies to make your dog walks more enjoyable while you practice the exercises in this book. If your dog is a big puller or there is a risk of neck injury due to pulling, look at the **Product Recommendations** section of this book and purchase an appropriate harness.

THE MOST IMPORTANT LEASH WALKING CONCEPTS

Dogs naturally walk faster than us. Expecting them to walk at our pace and ignore everything around them is a tall order and takes a lot of practice. Here are some overall concepts that will help speed up your training.

- If you have two dogs, work with them individually at least sometimes.
- Be more interesting than the environment. Use toys, treats, movement and your voice to make yourself more interesting than anything else. Be goofy and exciting.
- Use "Outside Only" toys that you reserve for walks. Keep squeaky toys, tug toys, and other fun objects and have them magically appear when your dog appears at your side.
- Use a long leash for leash walking practice. Hold your dog's leash, walk away and when she appears by your side, 'click' and treat. Continue walking and repeat. The

goal is for your dog to see you walking away and feel motivated to appear by your side because that is where treats and toys will appear.

WHEN SHOULD YOU PRACTICE OBEDIENCE?

I always suggest prioritizing desensitization over obedience in new situations. If you are working on leash walking strategies and you see a dog approaching, stop focusing on leash walking and switch to desensitization. Position yourself with your dog in between you and the other dog, 'click' and treat as the dog walks by or practice the movement strategies explained in this book if your dog is over threshold.

Once your dog is calm after moving to a new location, continue obedience. The long-term goal is that your dog doesn't react to other dogs and you can work on obedience in any situation since your dog doesn't react in an undesired way. You can always attempt to ask your dog to, "Leave It," "Watch Me," "Come," "Sit" or any other command at any point in your work near other dogs. However, if your dog simply is too distracted to perform those commands then you should adjust your expectations and switch to desensitization or move him away and practice obedience elsewhere.

LOOSE LEASH STRATEGIES

Two loose leash concepts that I want all dogs to know:

- When they feel a tight leash, they cannot continue walking.
- When they see the person holding the leash walking away, they should follow.

The consistent message is that when a dog feels a tight leash, she should make a different decision. It is your job to teach your dog what the proper decisions are. Practice the three following exercises to achieve this goal. You can practice any of these exercises throughout the day. You should practice inside and outside. When you are inside, put your dog on leash, place something on the floor or use it when someone is at the front door and work on these exercises. Allow your dog to gain access to the toy, food bowl or person when they are either looking back at you or walking with a loose leash.

It is very important to be proactive and notice when your dog is walking nicely before they start pulling. It is common to ignore good behavior and only start interacting with a dog once they pull. Notice good behaviors before pulling occurs and give feedback, "Good!" or 'click' and treat.

THREE LEASH WALKING EXERCISES

- Stop and Go
- Easy
- Changes In Direction

Try using toys as a reward on walks. I like to have "outside only" toys that only appear when a dog performs a good behavior. A quick game of tug can also be very rewarding. If your dog prefers treats, use treats.

STOP AND GO
Practice this inside your home, in front of your home and on your walks.
- Put your dog on leash.
- 'Click' and treat before pulling starts.
- As soon as she pulls, stop walking.
- Wait a bit to see if she changes her behavior.
- 'Click' and treat for any of the following behaviors.
  - Turning her head towards you
  - Walking toward you
  - Walking next to you
- If you do not see a behavior change after five to ten seconds, prompt your dog by making a "Nn," "Nn," noise with your mouth, tap your leg or kneel down a bit to entice your dog to move towards you.
- As soon as your dog performs one behavior above, 'click' and treat and then take a few steps forward.
- If your dog pulls, repeat the exercise.
- If your dog stops taking treats or is simply too distracted, work closer to home or inside your home.

EASY
I use "Easy" to ask dogs to slow down. You can use a 'click' and a treat when your dog performs this command. I typically just

use a verbal reinforcer "Good" and allow the dog to get closer to what interests them. You can think about anything your dog wants as a reward, including access to sniffing a tree, a treat on the floor, a guest at the front door or their food bowl.

Before the leash becomes tight, give your dog notice they are walking too far ahead of you - "Easy." As soon as the leash becomes taut, stop them gently or gently pull them back a couple of inches. This is not a rough movement and should not be unpleasant for your dog.

- Put your dog on leash.
- Start walking.
- When your dog gets ahead of you, say, "Easy."
- Either gently pull your arm back until the leash becomes taut or wait for the leash to become taut.
- Gently stop your dog's movement or guide your dog back a few inches.
- Say, "Good" and continue walking.

You can either stop moving after you say, "Easy" or continue walking the entire time while you are gently pulling the leash back. This is not a quick fix. Each time you take your dog on a walk, there are fresh smells and distractions. You need to practice leash walking strategies in new locations until your dog has generalized to all locations. This can take time. Be patient.

CHANGES IN DIRECTION

This strategy is useful if your dog is just not paying attention to anything. I use it to get a dog back on track and then I typically use the two other strategies more frequently. I mostly use verbal praise and rarely use treats during this exercise since there is a lot of movement and it is challenging to do so. Once a dog walks next to me, I will start using treats or toys again.

- Put your dog on leash.
- Start walking.
- AS SOON as your dog takes one step ahead of you, say, "This Way", change direction and GENTLY guide your dog with you. This is NOT a rough, jerking movement.
- As your dog appears by your side, use verbal praise. "Good job . . . this is where I want you to walk!" The point of this interaction is you are providing feedback and letting your dog know that if she walks next to you, she can continue walking forward.
- Most likely she will perform a "flyby" and charge ahead of you each time you change directions. That is expected. Make sure you give her lots of verbal praise while she is next to and stop the praise and change directions when she is ahead of you.
- Continue this process by changing direction and saying, "This Way" each time your dog walks one step ahead of you.

Yes, you might get a little dizzy. Be careful. The reason I think this exercise is successful is your dog will think, "What is going on? Where are we going?" and looks up at you and starts paying more attention. When you have your dog's attention, you can use verbal praise, 'clicks' and treats, give her a favorite toy, etc. Make that location the *fun zone*. She walks next to you and all kinds of fun stuff happens.

SUMMARY

- Movement and positioning strategies can be practiced with long leashes when you have enough space to maintain a safe distance from other dogs.
- For dogs that have a prey drive, a combination of desensitization and "Stop" are effective strategies.
- When working with leash walking strategies, it is recommended to prioritize desensitization when encountering new situations or other dogs.
- Practice desensitization in new situations.
- Once your dog is not distracted by the environment, obedience is much more likely to be successful.
- If your dog is too distracted for obedience, switch to desensitization or move her to a new location where she is less distracted.

Chapter 18
WORK OUTSIDE OF DOG PARKS

🐾

Whether your dog plays with other dogs in dog parks or not, you can use dogs that your dog sees both inside and outside the park to desensitize your dog.

To practice this effectively and avoid uncomfortable situations, the same rules apply as before. If your dog is too stressed, you need to move him to a location where he can be calm and respond to the 'click.' If you don't have enough space to find a neutral distance, then that is not a suitable location to practice.

If your dog is agitated five feet from the dog park fence, move fifteen or twenty feet away. Start at a completely neutral distance where your dog immediately responds to the 'click' and takes the treat or is interested in playing with toys.

Maybe your dog does not take treats at any distance. If so, you can still work near the dogs in the park by moving your dog back and forth nearby. But remember, this may not be effective if your dog gets more agitated or if the other dogs are barking and do not calm down. If this happens, there is too much stimulation and you should work somewhere else farther away from the park.

One benefit of dog parks is that once your dog has had lots of practice in other situations and has shown improvement, you can use the fence at dog parks to allow your dog to safely sniff other dogs.

Practice the **Click, Move, Treat** strategy when your dog is close enough to sniff other dogs until you have more experience with safe interactions. At that point, you can allow your dog to sniff for longer periods of time. Even though there is a fence, there is still a risk of causing physical injury or mental stress to your dog or the dogs in the park if you try too much too soon.

If your dog simply is too distracted to take treats, continuous movement is the safest option for introductions. Instead of letting them sniff nose-to-nose for five seconds and crossing your fingers, do a quick "fly-by" and after a quick sniff, keep moving your dog past the other dog. Evaluate both of the dog's reactions and decide if they can sniff for a few more seconds during the next interaction.

You also have to be aware of the physical characteristics of your dog and the dogs in the park. Long-nosed dogs like Greyhounds, Whippets, Borzois, small dogs or puppies might get their noses through the fence. They might bite your dog or get bitten if your dog bites. I am extra cautious around puppies when I am working with reactive dogs. The last thing in the world I want to happen is to traumatize a puppy with a snapping or biting dog. I avoid close interactions with puppies unless I am extremely confident about the stability of the dog that I am working with.

GOOD OFF LEASH BUT HAS ON-LEASH AGGRESSION?

If your dog can play off leash but is aggressive on-leash, use the dog park strategically to fix this problem. Frustration is the emotion that is causing problems. Your dog is used to seeing dogs and immediately playing with them. When he can't immediately get to the dogs because of the leash, he becomes frustrated and reactive as he approaches the dog park.

Clients have hired me many times over the years to help leash reactive dogs that safely go to daycare, or frequently visit dog parks. The dog was not taught to be calm around dogs, and to understand seeing a dog is not a guarantee of play.

"Why can't I go play with those dogs, NOW!"

If you can teach him to be patient and eliminate the frustration, the aggression will go away. The key is to teach him that just because dogs are in view, he doesn't automatically get to play.

Start slow and avoid the build-up of frustration as much as possible. If he can play off leash safely, let him play with dogs at the start of this exercise to satisfy his desire and tire him out, reducing his need for dog interaction.

Note: Taking treats into a dog park can cause dogs to follow you, possibly fight over treats, or annoy fellow owners. You might want to leave your treats outside of the park.

TRY THIS:
BEGINNER
1. Go directly into the dog park and let your dog play for five to ten minutes to get him tired and give him his dog "fix."
2. Take him out of the dog park.
3. Find a distance away from the park and practice five 'clicks' and treats. Each time you should be at a distance where he turns towards the 'click' immediately and takes the treat.
4. Go back into the dog park and let him play for five to ten minutes.
5. Come out of the park and do five successful 'clicks' and treats. A successful 'click' and treat is when your dog

turns around immediately and takes the treat gently. Move to a location where this occurs.

6. Repeat this process every five to ten minutes for as long as you are at the park.

INTERMEDIATE

Move to this step once your dog becomes calmer when approaching the park. Work outside of the dog park for five successful 'clicks' and treats before you go into the dog park. Everything else is the same as the beginning version.

1. Then go into the dog park and let your dog play for five to ten minutes.
2. Take him out of the dog park.
3. Find a distance away from the park and practice five 'clicks' and treats. Each time you should be at a distance where he turns towards the 'click' immediately and takes the treat.
4. Go back into the dog park and let him play for five to ten minutes.
5. Come out of the park and do five successful 'clicks' and treats.
6. Repeat this process every five to ten minutes for as long as you are at the park.

ADVANCED

When your dog is calm walking up to the dog park gate.

This should be your ultimate goal. You can go to the dog park, have your dog calmly walk up to the gate, and he should remain calm. If he sees dogs coming or going out of the park, he should not react. You can decide whether he actually goes into the park and plays with dogs or maybe you take him for a walk near the park. Either way, he should be calm and not frustrated.

Before you reach your ultimate goal, your dog should be calmer. You might notice that he pulls less towards the park, or he turns towards you when he sees dogs instead of dragging you. This can take many sessions to reach this goal.

SUMMARY

- Dog parks can help with desensitization.
- Use other dogs strategically to desensitize your dog to seeing other dogs, whether or not they play in dog parks.
- Frustration is the root cause of reactivity for dogs that play safely off leash. If your dog is used to seeing and interacting with other dogs, he will feel frustrated when denied immediate access.
- Use the "Click, Move, Treat" strategy to introduce your dog to other dogs, starting with brief interactions and gradually making them longer.
- If your dog remains calm at the dog park gate and doesn't react to other dogs, you have successfully desensitized them.
- Be cautious when bringing treats into the park or leave them outside the park.

Chapter 19
PRODUCT RECOMMENDATIONS

🐾

Here are some product recommendations. Ultimately, you need to decide what products you are comfortable with, but I have found the following options to work best.

LEASH RECOMMENDATION
- Six foot leash (not a retractable)
  - My preference is leather, but climbing rope, cotton or nylon work too.
  - Leash should have a handle at the end to put your hand through.
  - Some leashes have an extra handle close to the dog for holding on to if you need more support. They can be helpful for really powerful dogs.
  - Width of 1/2 inch is acceptable for small dogs or 3/4 inch for medium or large dogs. Leather one inch leashes can still be very comfortable, but a well made 3/4 inch is strong enough for any dog.

WHY NOT A RETRACTABLE LEASH?
I have never met a trainer that likes retractable leashes. I don't like them at all. Retractable leashes are especially not suitable for reactive dogs or dogs that are not well-trained on a leash.

- Retractable leashes are always tight. I want dogs to learn that if there is a tight leash, they should slow down.
- They limit your ability to control your dog since they require one hand carrying the big plastic handle.
- They can tangle around other leashes and dogs.
- If you don't lock the retractable leash properly, your dog may reach another dog when you believe you locked the leash at a short length, which can be disastrous.
- If you drop the handle, it can scare your dog as they are trying to run away from the handle, bouncing on the ground behind them.
- You also can't work on obedience like you can work on with a fixed length long leash. I use long leashes frequently in lengths of twelve, fifteen, twenty, thirty and fifty feet. Once a dog is under control in a safe situation, you can drop the long leash on the ground and have him trail it. You can then work on behaviors such as "Come" and gently stop your dog with the leash if needed. You can't do that with a retractable.

CHOKE, PRONG OR SHOCK COLLAR?

Don't use a choke, prong or shock collar. They add pain, they can cause fear and they are unnecessary. Physical punishment is never a good idea. I don't recommend or use any of these punishers. One of the many reasons I don't use physical punishment is that you can increase anxiety by associating pain with the appearance of a trigger. If your dog associates other dogs with pain from barking and lunging while wearing a choke chain or shock collar, he may become anxious around them.

You can also train signals out of a dog. If your dog barks and has a painful experience with a choke or shock, he can stop barking or showing other signals since it resulted in pain. Then, you can end up with a dog that is anxious and doesn't give signals. That is a dangerous dog. You can't tell when he is comfortable or anxious. He can bite quickly without warning. Sometimes we cannot rehabilitate dogs that do not give signals.

COLLARS

A regular, flat collar is fine if your dog is not gagging when pulling on it. If he is, he can end up with throat or trachea damage. Instead, switch to a harness or head halter.

For Greyhounds or other long-necked, small headed breeds, often the best collar option is a martingale or limited-slip collar. This tightens on the neck but doesn't choke like a choke or prong collar.

HARNESS

There are many brands or styles, but the two options comprise connecting the leash on the back of your dog or in the front near the chest. For small dogs or dogs that don't pull, either option is fine. If your dog thinks he is trying out for the Iditarod and walks are unmanageable, use a front harness.

If you attach the leash to the back, dogs can use their entire body to pull. Front attachments give you leverage by turning your dog's body around if they pull. There are many front attachment harnesses, but I usually recommend either the Sensible or Senseation Harness. You can visit my Product Recommendations Page where you can find harnesses and other useful products that I use. www.jeffmillman.com.

The front harnesses that have more padding are becoming more prevalent, but they often are not tight enough and slide around more. The only downside to the harnesses mentioned above is that for short-haired dogs, they can sometimes cause abrasions. Unless they change the Senseation and add more padding, I suggest adding cotton squares and sports tape to the belly strap to make it more comfortable. I know this sounds like a lot of work, but it is really an excellent product and is worth the extra effort. Medium and long-haired dogs don't require extra padding. Always get the wider strap version, if available. It is much more comfortable.

HEAD HALTER

In the past, head halters such as the Halti or Gentle Leader were more commonly used. They are generally considered effective and humane. However, many dogs dislike them and will spend most of the walk scratching at them and might roll around in the grass in frustration.

SUMMARY

- Use a 6-foot leash (not retractable).
- Preferred materials include leather, climbing rope, cotton, or nylon.
- Consider a leash with an extra handle close to the dog for better control with powerful dogs.
- Avoid choke, prong, or shock collars as they cause pain and unnecessary fear.
- Front-attachment harnesses offer better control for strong pullers and larger dogs.
- Front harnesses with more padding can ease rubbing problems, but can slip and not be as effective. When using the Sensible or Senseation with short-haired dogs, cotton squares and sports tape can improve comfort.

Chapter 20
TROUBLESHOOTING

YOUR DOG DOESN'T TAKE TREATS

First, conduct a baseline assessment and make sure they like the treats inside in a non-threatening environment. If they take treats inside, but not outside, it means they are immediately over-threshold. You need to work slowly and get them used to as many triggers as possible, including noises.

If they simply do not usually like treats, experiment with different food sources. A Rottweiler I worked with liked Oyster Crackers more than roast beef.

If they stop taking treats on a walk, it means they are distracted or nervous. Stop using the clicker so they don't start ignoring it. If they are functioning normally and not too stressed, continue working with them and periodically offer a treat. When they take treats again, you can start using the clicker again.

YOUR DOG SNAPS OR BITES WITHOUT WARNING

Take this extremely seriously and be extra cautious. Consider a muzzle for any location where you are not 100% confident that you can stay at a safe distance. If you live in an elevator building, your dog should wear a muzzle until you are safely outside, and also take the stairs, if possible.

This behavior indicates a high level of anxiety and potential reactivity with multiple triggers. Talk to your veterinarian about anti-anxiety medication. Once your dog is not reacting so intensely, he might show warning signals. Extreme caution needs to be taken with this type of reactivity. This is one of the most challenging types of dog aggression.

TOY, STICK OR OTHER GUARDING AT PARKS
A dog that guards toys or other objects should NOT be off leash around other dogs unless it is in a backyard or other controlled environment with a strict NO TOY policy. Many fights at dog parks occur because a dog is guarding something.

CONTINUOUS WHINING OR BARKING OUTSIDE
This can happen if a dog has generalized anxiety. They get nervous inside in anticipation of being outside. Certain dogs may require anti-anxiety medication to reduce their baseline anxiety and promote calmness. Whether or not your dog is on medication, try 'clicking' and treating before you go outside, and immediately when you go outside. Assuming your dog is taking treats, this is a starting point for progress. After you achieve a few 'clicks' and treats outside, go back inside, let your dog decompress and then try again. If you have twenty minutes for a walk, you might go in and out multiple times during that time. The goals are that you relieve the stress and distract your dog with treats before they get anxious.

REDIRECTED AGGRESSION WITH TWO DOGS

If you have two dogs and one or both attacks the other when a trigger is present, you need to walk them separately. That indicates a high level of stress, anxiety, and frustration. If a dog cannot interact with something immediately, they can get frustrated. If it results in an attack, the overall anxiety and frustration is so high that you cannot expect to make any progress in that situation. You should lower the reactivity to triggers for each dog before expecting them to be calm when walked together. Also consider discussing anti-anxiety medication options with your veterinarian if you do not see results.

AFRAID OF MULTIPLE TRIGGERS DURING WALKS

If your dog constantly reacts, and you're not making progress, consider some options.

- Isolate the various triggers (skateboards, dogs, joggers, delivery trucks, etc.) and try to work on each separately. Have a family member push a skateboard back and forth at a distance where your dog responds to the 'click.' Use recordings of delivery trucks and other triggers and play them at a level that your dog takes treats and is calm.
- Walk your dog in a quieter area more frequently. Each time your dog gets agitated, it is more likely he will get agitated during the next walk.

ELEVATOR BUILDING DANGERS

If you live in an elevator building and you have a reactive dog, you have a few options to increase safety.

- Put a muzzle on your dog before you leave your home and use it in the hallway, elevator, stairs and lobby.
- Take the stairs with your dog muzzled, or take the elevator while using a muzzle if you there are too many flights of stairs.
- Remove the muzzle, if it is safe to do so, when you are out of the building away from people and dogs.

CONSIDER ANTI-ANXIETY MEDICATION

If your dog reacts strongly to daily triggers, it may be challenging or impossible to reduce their reactivity through desensitization alone. Anti-anxiety medication can lower reactivity, allowing you to find a starting point to help desensitize your dog to triggers.

I urge you not to consider medication as a *last resort*. What does that mean? Your dog bites five more people? You can't walk your dog any longer? You are at your wit's end? Sometimes dogs simply need to lower stress levels and medication is not a new, unproven science. Find a skilled veterinarian and ask for their guidance. My clients have had the most luck with Prozac (generic Fluoxetine) but there are many good options out there. I have not had good luck with Trazadone for daily reactivity. That can be useful for vet visits or other situational uses.

The proper medication does not change your dog's overall personality. Medication simply adjusts a dog's chemical balance and lowers their stress and reactivity. The changes that you will see will be subtle and gradual. You still need to work diligently on desensitization strategies once your dog starts medication.

Here are some red flags that might indicate your dog needs medication. Some of the criteria, such as if your dog bites and especially if he bites without warning, might be all it takes for you to make this decision. Treating your dog without medication can be very challenging if they show one or more of these characteristics.

- Your dog reacts intensely frequently on walks.
- Your dog continuously barks or whines during walks.
- Your dog reacts aggressively at thirty feet or more.
- Your dog redirects his aggression towards you or your other dog when he sees a trigger.
- Your dog does not give warning signals before extreme agitation or a bite.
- Your dog has bitten dogs or people.
- Your dog has one or more severe bites resulting in puncture wounds, stitches or hospital visits.
- Your dog has multiple triggers such as people, dogs, or skateboards.
- Your dog also shows other issues such as separation anxiety or resource guarding.

- Your dog has difficulty calming down after a barking incident, indicating an extreme level of agitation. This is called *poor recovery*.
- Your dog quickly goes over threshold and stops taking treats.
- Your dog's reactivity is getting worse.

I recommend medication if your dog's aggression severely affects your family and dog's quality of life. You can't board your dog because he is aggressive. You can't have holiday gatherings at your home because your dog is dangerous. Your dog is not getting proper exercise and you can't walk your dog outside. By reducing stress levels, your dog can become the best possible version of himself with the help of medication. He will also be easier to manage and you hopefully can start taking him places, which will make him more relaxed and tired.

Medication is not a silver bullet. It does not cause a quick or immediate change in your dog's reactivity. You should work with a skilled positive reinforcement dog trainer to continue working on the desensitization strategies in this book. You will also still need to practice rock-solid management strategies to keep your dog away from people and dogs and keep everyone safe.

WHY DO SOME BREEDS HAVE MORE CHALLENGES?
Some breeds like Akitas, German Shepherds, Shiba Inus, Pit Bulls, French Bulldogs, Malinois, Boxers, Rottweilers, and

others may struggle with socializing or going to dog parks. They are all intense, very athletic dogs with specific play styles, such as using their paws or bodies during play. Many dogs take issue with these types of interactions and often don't want to interact or will get defensive and reactive.

For example, Akitas begin as fluffy fur balls, but quickly grow into mammoth, powerful dogs that intimidate most other dogs. They also have a natural guarding and territorial nature. Even if you socialize an Akita perfectly, there is a small population of dogs that will feel comfortable interacting with these giants. This leads to an Akita not receiving enough socialization with other dogs. If that Akita also gets agitated behind a window or fence, the reactivity will be more pronounced. This combination is not looking good for calm, uneventful greetings with other dogs.

I have had many conversations with clients pointing out that their bouncy puppy plays beautifully with other dogs right now, but their dog park visits might be numbered as their dog gets older. Many clients reach out to me when their dog is older, informing me that they no longer attend open play sessions and only have play dates with familiar dogs, or avoid off leash play completely.

If your dog is too intense for other dogs, you have a few options:

- Find dogs that have a similar size and play style as your dog and schedule play dates in a backyard.
- Stop bringing your dog to dog parks and find other outlets such as structured fly ball, agility, tracking, scent work or herding.
- Use a long leash or find a safe off-leash location and play frisbee or fetch.
- Take your dog for hikes and long walks in new locations to provide novel sensory experiences.
- Practice more obedience training to ensure your dog is not bored.

INTACT MALES GETTING TARGETED

If you get your dog from a shelter, this might not be a concern, since many shelters will not adopt a dog without spaying or neutering. But, if you get your male dog from a breeder, you need to decide if/when you get him neutered. Most veterinarians recommend waiting at least a year or more.

This can create challenges if your dog interacts with other male dogs. Even other dogs that are neutered can target and bully intact males in social settings, sometimes resulting in a fight. I stopped going to dog parks with my dog, Sky, when he was eight months old because he was getting tormented by a group of male dogs. After neutering him a few months later, we returned to the dog park, and the dogs walked away after a quick greeting. Their demeanor towards him completely changed.

Chapter 21
FREQUENTLY ASKED QUESTIONS

🐾

Q: You mentioned the clicker is like a camera. Can you explain that a bit more?

A: Sure. The clicker is a marker and an easy way to think of it is that is a camera taking a picture. You are doing one of two things:

1. **Taking a picture of an event** to help your dog enjoy that experience and evaluate how your dog responds. When you are *taking a picture of an event*, notice when your dog sees or hears something, 'click' at that exact moment and evaluate your dog's response. If he is not concerned about the event, he will ignore it, turn around and eat the treat. Not only will he enjoy that event more since it results in treats, but you can evaluate how he responds to the 'click.' If he is stressed, move him away and work at a less intense distance.

2. **Taking a picture of a behavior** that your dog performs to precisely teach him what the behavior is and to motivate him to do the behavior more frequently. When you are using the clicker this way, you are *taking a*

picture of a behavior to precisely teach your dog what you want him to do. It makes teaching much easier because of the precision of the 'click.' The 'click' happens while the behavior is happening.

Q: Is the clicker is used to distract my dog?

A: The strategy is to see *if* the clicker can distract him, not use the clicker *to* distract him. I focus on evaluating a dog's response to the clicker to see if he is calm or anxious. It will distract your dog *if* he can be distracted from what he is looking at. Since your dog knows the 'click' means a treat is behind his head, if he ignores the 'click,' it means that he is interested or nervous about something else.

If he usually barks at other dogs and keeps looking at the other dog rather than turning towards the 'click,' it likely means he's about to bark at that dog. These undesired behaviors can occur whether he is nervous or simply excited. If he turns his attention away from the other dog, it means he isn't concerned and won't bark or get frustrated. Desensitization involves controlled exposure to stressors until dogs no longer react negatively. A calm dog doesn't react, a dog that is stressed does.

Just imagine if you were walking to your car late at night with a friend in a parking lot. You hear an unusual noise and think it might be a person following you. This makes you nervous, and then your friend asks you to look at a funny video on her phone. Would you be calm enough to ignore the potential threat and enjoy the funny video? Would you be able to be distracted away from the unknown person? Nope. You would inform your friend that there is something more important that you need to pay attention to at that moment. Once you felt safe, you could focus on the funny puppy video on her phone.

The same concept applies to dogs. If they are too distracted, they have more important things to do than look towards the 'click' and eat the treat.

Using the strategies in this book, you are evaluating the very primal responses that your dog has to the world around him. If he isn't calm, move him somewhere else and continue working.

Q: I can also use the clicker for obedience? Won't that be confusing to my dog?

A: No, not a problem at all. You can also use the clicker for obedience. Focus first on the emotional response to a trigger.

Once your dog is calm and is not concerned with the trigger, then you can work on obedience. Your dog is always having emotional responses and learning, you cannot separate the two:

- When you are training, your dog is also having fun. (Learning first, emotions second).
- When he gets surprised and reacts to a scary rumbling noise, he is also learning that firetrucks are scary. (Emotions first, learning second).

However, you can prioritize your focus. If your dog is in a brand new situation, that is not the ideal time to teach him something brand new. Work on his emotional responses first. 'Click' and treat when your dog notices the surrounding triggers, including dogs, people, bicycles, traffic, etc. If your dog can ignore distractions and respond to the click by turning towards you, it means they are calm and ready to learn.

Q: Everything I have read or trainer I spoke with previously told me that when my dog is barking at another dog, I should ask him to "Heel" or "Leave it" or "Sit." Why don't you recommend that?

A: That is what most trainers will tell you. That concept lies in the strategy of an incompatible behavior. If a dog is walking next to you and looking up at you doing a perfect heel, then he can't bark at the dog ten feet away, correct? If that is working, by all means, that is a fantastic idea.

Instead, my philosophy addresses the problem of what if a dog is too anxious or distracted to perform that behavior? I want a dog to be aware of all of the triggers in his space and not feel threatened because he is worried that dog will attack him or frustrated because he can't interact with that dog. I focus on preventing reactions instead of correcting a dog's behavior.

If I ask for a "Leave It" or other behavior and the dog simply isn't able to do that behavior, I will try one of two strategies:

- Move the dog away from the trigger and ask for the behavior at a farther location.
- Move the dog away from the trigger and work on desensitization by 'clicking' and treating when he looks at the trigger at a farther location.

After either option above, you should be able to move closer to the trigger and continue working on either one of those strategies until you achieve your goal. Eventually you should be able to practice obedience in any situation as long as your dog is comfortable.

It is very easy to blame a dog for not "behaving," when in fact, he is just too nervous or distracted. I focus on first introducing dogs to new things and evaluating their response. If they are comfortable in that situation, let the obedience exercises begin! We should prioritize calming the dog and desensitizing him to the triggers, causing undesired responses.

Q: I have heard mixed reviews about dog parks. What do you think about them?

A: Bring up dog parks around dog people and you will definitely get some powerful responses. My answer is that, in theory, they are amazing. You take your dog to a park, let her run around with a bunch of dogs and then you have a happy, tired dog and you can get a lot of work done that day. In reality, they can be filled with hazards. Sick dogs, dogs that guard sticks and toys, unsocialized dogs, etc.

In Chicago, I frequently took my dogs to dog parks and worked with clients there as well. They are almost a necessity since few people have back yards to exercise their dogs. When I moved to North Carolina, I brought Sky to dog parks frequently, but had some unpleasant experiences. I decided that our next puppy, Storm, is not a dog park dog. Instead, I schedule play dates with friends in our backyard and am very picky who I let him interact with on walks. So far, we have found that it works for us and Storm is well socialized and happy. You need to decide what is best for you and your dog.

I have suggestions about dog parks:

- Discuss dog parks with your veterinarian. If they have lots of injured dogs from nearby parks, avoid those parks.

- Be aware of outbreaks of dog flu, Parvo or other illnesses. Check with your veterinarian about these topics as well. Even if you go to dog parks, avoid them if there is an outbreak.

- Be careful if you have an intact dog. You don't want a surprise litter if you have a female dog and your intact male dog might get into fights as he matures. There will probably be a time that you take a break or stop going to dog parks as your dog matures.

- Survey the park before you go in. If you see an aggressive dog that is starting fights, don't go in.

- Look at the numbers of dogs. I would never go into a park with over ten dogs and ideally only five. I have seen dog parks that have thirty or more dogs. That is a dog fight waiting to happen. Go during quiet times or find another outlet for your dog.

- Consider your breed and temperament of a dog. If you have a more intense dog such as a German Shepherd, Pit Bull, Boxer, Min Pin, Akita, American Bull Dog, etc, you have to be extra careful in dog park settings. Even high-energy small dogs such as Boston Terriers can get into fights. Some dogs will not back down if there is an altercation or their play style causes other dogs to fight. If your dog bullies other dogs, find another outlet.

- If you have a puppy or small dog, only go to dog parks if there is a separate small dog area.
- Make sure you desensitize your dog to dogs by using the strategies in the **Dog Parks** section of this book. You want your dog to understand that just because she sees a dog does not mean she always gets to play.
- Consider scheduling play dates with dog friends instead of dog parks.
- If your dog doesn't interact with other dogs when at the dog park, don't waste your time going to dog parks. It means your dog is probably not having fun.
- Don't go to dog parks if your dog is afraid. Going there will make the situation worse.

Q: Are dog daycares a good option to socialize and provide exercise for my dog?

A: Assuming your dog can safely interact with other dogs off leash, do your research and make an informed decision. I have talked to clients that have taken their dog to daycare for years with no problems and others that go once and end up at the emergency vet. Use your judgment, check reviews, etc.

Other considerations for daycare:
- Try to find one that provides video footage of play time.
- Get to the know the staff and ask a lot of questions.
- How do they decide which dogs to accept? (Temperament testing).

Triggers and Reactions   On-Leash Aggression

- How do they decide which dogs to play with each other? Size, age, energy level, etc.
- What if there is an outbreak of flu or other illness? Do they tell all the dog owners?
- Is there structured downtime?
- What does the downtime look like? Are dogs in crates?
- What is their procedure for breaking up a dog fight? Are dogs allowed back after that?
- How long have the staff members worked there? (A lot of turnover could be a bad sign).
- Don't overdo it. Five days a week might be too much. Full days might be too much. Half days two days a week might be all your dog needs.
- See if your dog has trouble relaxing after day care. Tired is good. Overstimulated is not.
- Daycare staff might pet your jumping dog, leading to obedience problems at home. Talk to them if you see behavior changes.

Q: My dog barks out of the window and in my backyard. Should I worry about this?

A: Absolutely. Usually when a client hires me for leash aggression, their dog also barks out of the window or in the backyard. This feeds into a dog's frustration and reactivity. It is called *Barrier Frustration* and will make on-leash aggression treatment more difficult. Keep your dog away from the

171

window when you can't monitor him and 'click' and treat every time your dog looks out of the window.

Whether your dog is by a window or outdoors, apply the techniques in this book to treat reactivity. Don't use the clicker when your dog is barking. Move him away to a location where he stops barking, then 'click' and treat when he looks at or hears the trigger.

Q: My dog doesn't always respond to the clicker when he sees a dog. Should I keep clicking until he responds?

A: No. Think of the clicker to ask your dog, "What do you think about what you are looking at?" If he doesn't care about what he is looking at, he will turn around after one 'click.' The clicker is one way to gather information about your dog's mental state. If he doesn't turn around after one click, that is all the information you need. Move him to a new location and work at a farther distance by 'clicking' and treating once he looks back at the other dog.

Q: One member of the family doesn't want to use the clicker. Is that going to confuse my dog?

A: No, it will be fine. As long as every member of the family is consistent in their training. One person can also use the clicker and another can primarily use "Yes!" instead.

Q: What if I forget the clicker at home?

A: You always have your voice. Use "Yes!" instead. The clicker is louder and more consistent, however, so you probably find that it works better. If you forget treats, then just give your dog a nice brisk walk and try to avoid triggers that typically cause your dog to get agitated.

Q: My dog is afraid of the clicker. What should I do?

A: You can muffle it in your pocket or under your arm, or use "Yes!" instead. There are also various styles of clickers and some are much quieter. There are also apps that you can download on your phone and adjust the volume.

Q: My dog used to pay attention to the clicker but now he does not. What should I do?

A: You might have pushed him too fast. Make sure you are working at distances where he can be calm. Try shorter walks or stay closer to home. You should evaluate his stress levels around all triggers that he is exposed to. He might be stressed when he sees bicycles, trucks, joggers, or garage doors opening and closing. If many things cause him stress, he might be pushed out of his comfort zone and stop taking treats, which can result from *Compound Triggers*. If he has too much happening at one time, he might experience *Stacked Triggers*. You should also experiment with tastier treats and try walking him in other locations. If he stops responding to the clicker, stop using it and periodically offer him a treat during the walk. Once he takes treats again, you can probably start using the clicker again.

Q: Should I use a muzzle on my dog?

A: I would never advise someone not to use a muzzle. Besides avoiding the situation entirely, muzzles are the safest option for a reactive dog. However, there are some situations where a muzzle is a necessity if there is any concern about unpredictable behavior. The scenarios where muzzles make the most sense are:

*   a hallway, elevator, stairwell or lobby, with people and dogs
*   during a veterinarian visit
*   at the groomer
*   anywhere where you are not 100% sure your dog will not bite a person or dog

However, I think that muzzles can be used as a band-aid where avoidance is a better decision. Putting a muzzle on a dog, bringing her in public and causing stress can worsen her anxiety and make treatment more difficult. There are also some trainers that will put muzzles on dogs and let them interact off leash to see how they will react. This potentially has some value if the trainer is very skilled and used this strategy as a final safety measure after a lot of desensitization work. But, I don't recommend placing a dog in a situation that is untested or has resulted in a lot of stress if this situation can be avoided. I always err on the side of caution and practice desensitizing a dog to triggers and evaluate their responses first.

Q: My dog doesn't even look at other dogs. She just looks at me to get another treat. What should I do?

A: This is a good sign! It means:

- She has associated dogs with treats. Dogs = treats. Yay!
- You have done an amazing job and have chosen the correct distance and location for her to remain comfortable. Keep up the great work!
- She can perform obedience commands in that situation since she is not feeling threatened by the other dog.
- In those situations, you can rely more on verbal praise instead of using treats, as she is emotionally stable and consistent in her responses and behaviors.

Q: My dog seems calm but then barks or lunges randomly. What does that mean?

A: This means that when your dog seems calm, he is actually experiencing stress. If a dog reacts when a dog is five feet away, he was already nervous ten, fifteen or twenty feet away. Be more conservative with your distances, monitor your dog's stress levels, and click and treat frequently. You should also discuss anti-anxiety medication options with your veterinarian.

ABOUT THE AUTHOR

Jeff Millman is a certified professional dog trainer with over twenty one years dog training and consulting experience. He obtained his Bachelor of Arts in Journalism and Art from Indiana University in Bloomington, IN. Following a successful career as a creative director, he pursued his lifelong dream of working with animals. He transitioned to his career in dog training after studying with Jean Donaldson at the Academy for Dog Trainers in San Francisco, CA in 2002, where he graduated with honors.

He has owned two successful dog training businesses and was a consultant to a large corporation where he helped establish a Bring Your Dog to Work program. Jeff has also worked as a behavior consultant for an animal rescue organization.

He currently has a thriving private dog training business and lives in North Carolina with his amazing wife, two incredible children and the sweetest English Shepherds, Sky and Storm.

www.ingramcontent.com/pod-product-compliance
Lightning Source LLC
Chambersburg PA
CBHW072237270326
41930CB00010B/2168